JAZZ**BLUES**SOLOING
FOR**GUITAR**

A Guitarist's Guide to Playing the Changes on a Jazz Blues

JOSEPH**ALEXANDER**

FUNDAMENTAL**CHANGES**

Jazz Blues Soloing for Guitar

A Guitarist's Guide to Playing the Changes on a Jazz Blues

Published by **www.fundamental-changes.com**

ISBN: 978-1-78933-041-0

Second Edition

Audio recorded by Pete Sklaroff

www.fundamental-changes.com

Twitter: @guitar_joseph

Over 10,000 fans on Facebook: **FundamentalChangesInGuitar**

Instagram: **FundamentalChanges**

For over 350 Free Guitar Lessons with Videos Check Out

www.fundamental-changes.com

Cover Image Copyright: Shutterstock: Richard Soliz

Contents

Introduction

The jazz blues is the most commonly called tune at any jam night. Its structure has been used to write hundreds of jazz standards, and because of its crossover between the standard 'Texas' 12-bar blues form and the more complex structures of jazz music, it is one of the most important pieces of repertoire to master for any student of jazz guitar.

The jazz blues is a 12-bar blues with a couple of harmonic twists and turns. Sometimes these twists can be taken to far-reaching extremes (for example, in Charlie Parker's Blues for Alice), but instead of seeing these additions as problems, jazz musicians see them as new opportunities to be expressive, find new melodies and break up the monotony of the standard 12-bar progression.

The chord changes in a jazz blues allow us to move away from the minor pentatonic vocabulary that is abundant in 'traditional' blues melodies and solos. This isn't to say that the minor pentatonic scale *isn't* used; it definitely is! However, by adding in new chords we can reach for new arpeggios, scales and *feelings* that the traditional I, IV, V, 12-bar blues doesn't allow us.

Interestingly, some of the more common 'jazzy' harmonic additions have made their way *back* into standard 12 blues repertoire. You will notice these as we explore the complexity of the jazz 12-bar structure throughout the book.

This book breaks down each section of the jazz blues chord structure and teaches the correct arpeggios, scales, substitutions and approaches available at each stage. We begin simply, but develop the essential first principles into complex, articulate devices that you can use over each chord.

This book has a practical focus on playing musical ideas which are naturally developed through understanding the fundamental principles of jazz. It is not simply a theory book, you will constantly see how every concept discussed can be used to create meaningful, articulate guitar solos.

Much of the information in this book is transferable to many other jazz structures and musical genres. Many of the lines will work over a traditional 12-bar blues too, so you will learn some great lines to pull out when you're jamming with your friends.

Throughout, the focus is on a meaningful transition from essential 'theoretical' principles, to playing musical jazz guitar solos on the blues form.

While not essential, I do highly recommend that you take a look at my book, **Fundamental Changes in Jazz Guitar**, as this prepares the groundwork for many of the approaches taken when learning to solo on any jazz standard.

Fundamental Changes in Jazz Guitar also goes into much more detail on the essential *major ii V I* chord progression than I have room to include here. One quarter of the jazz blues is formed from a major ii V I chord sequence, so a good understanding of this will be an advantage when working through this book.

I generally avoid talking about minor pentatonic soloing on the assumption that you already have a good grasp of its application on a 'normal' blues. This is not to say *don't* use the minor pentatonic scale, but focusing on learning the blues from a bebop perspective will greatly increase your musicianship. You will naturally find yourself adding minor pentatonic/blues scale ideas later, so try not to let yourself 'noodle' with the minor pentatonic instead of practicing.

It is important to internalise each concept and its associated vocabulary slowly, and make sure you're playing strong notes on strong beats. By building this solid foundation, you continually develop your ears, so that you can start to let go of 'the rules' later when you solo. You will begin to hear the melodies you wish to play, instead of sticking to the theory that you know you're 'allowed' to play.

While a huge part of this book is about teaching you appropriate scales and arpeggios, try to see the bigger picture, which is to view everything in this book as ear training. The truth is, that there are really no rights and wrongs in music. If it sounds good it is good. The point of this book is to give you access to new sounds.

Have fun,

Joseph

Note: Chapter One in this book deals with the construction and theory behind the jazz blues chord progression. While you will hopefully find it interesting, it is a little 'theory intensive' If you know how and why a jazz blues is formed, or you simply want to get to the soloing, please feel free to skip Chapter One!

Get the Audio

The audio files for this book are available to download for free from www.fundamental-changes.com. The link is in the top right-hand corner. Simply select this book title from the drop-down menu and follow the instructions to get the audio.

We recommend that you download the files directly to your computer, not to your tablet, and extract them there before adding them to your media library. You can then put them on your tablet, iPod or burn them to CD. On the download page there is a help PDF and we also provide technical support via the contact form.

For over 350 Free Lessons with Videos Check out:

www.fundamental-changes.com

Over 10,000 fans on Facebook: **FundamentalChangesInGuitar**

Instagram: **FundamentalChanges**

Chapter One - The Jazz Blues Structure

We will begin by looking at how jazz musicians developed the 'standard' 12-bar blues into a richer, more complex structure by using a simple convention in jazz.

For reference, here is the traditional 12-bar blues in the style of B.B. King or Howlin' Wolf:

Example 1a:

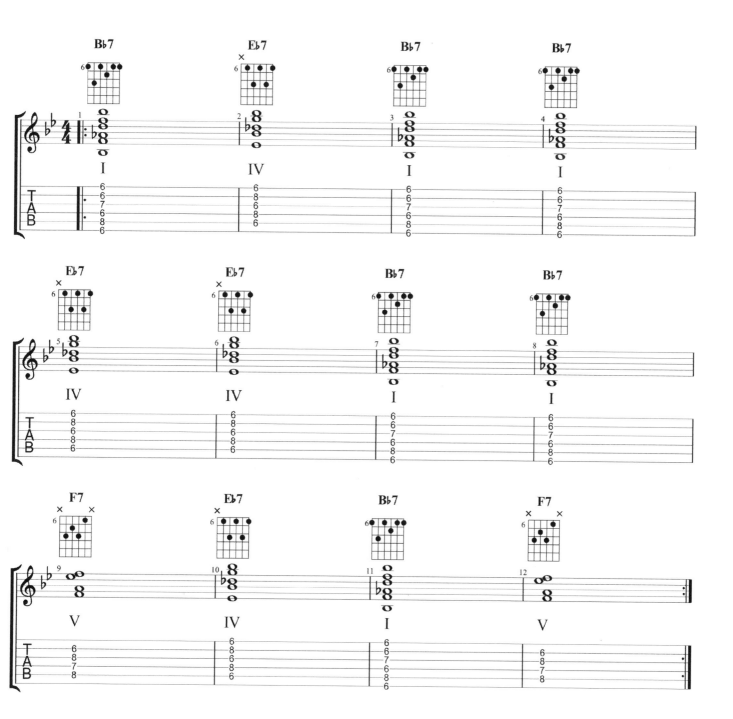

The Roman numeral analysis of each chord is written in below the stave. Chord one = I, Chord four = IV etc.

In jazz, it is common practice to precede any chord, by another chord that is a perfect 5th away. This chord can have *any* quality (7, maj7, min 7 etc.) but is *normally* a dominant 7. This sounds complicated when written down, so let's look at a simple example in the key of Bb.

Here is a simple chord sequence:

Example 1b:

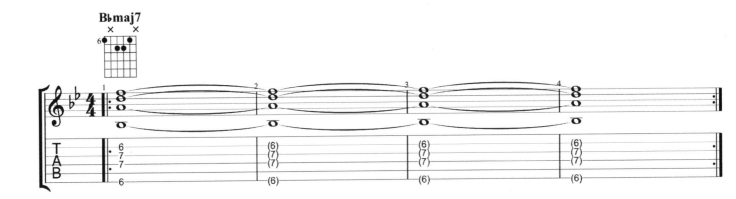

As far as jazz chord progressions go, it doesn't get much simpler than this.

Let's apply this idea, and precede the Bb7 by the chord that is a perfect 5th away from it. The chord that is a perfect fifth away is called the 'dominant chord'.

Count up through the scale: Bb, C, D, Eb, *F.*

The chord that is a perfect 5th above Bb7 is F. Play it as a dominant 7th chord.

Adding it to the chord progression, we create this repeating sequence:

Example 1c:

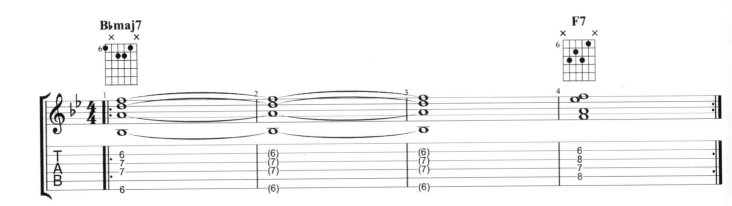

We can repeat the process and now add in the chord that is one 5th above F: C.

This time we will play it as a minor 7 chord (although there is no reason not to play it as a dominant chord).

Example 1d:

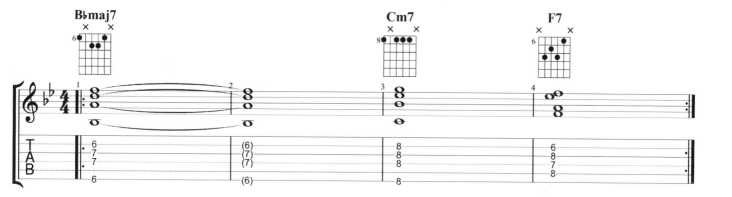

We have now created the most common chord sequence in jazz music; the major ii V I. Cm7 is chord ii of Bb, and F is chord V of Bb.

Let's go one step further and add in the dominant chord to Cm7. The dominant chord of Cm7 is G. You can count C, D, Eb F *G.* Once again, we will play this chord as a minor 7 chord.

Adding in the Gm7, our chord progression now looks like this:

Example 1e:

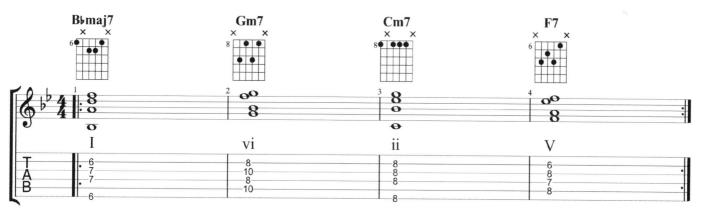

This chord sequence is often referred to as the I VI II V progression. It is another extremely common progressions in jazz.

Bb7 is chord I, Gm7 is chord VI, Cm7 is chord ii and F7 is chord V.

The reason I have chosen these specific chord qualities is because they are the qualities that are generated *naturally* when you harmonise the Bb major scale.

If you need a recap on this, I'd suggest you read my book **The Practical Guide to Modern Music Theory for Guitarists**.

For now, however, we shall quickly recap on the chords formed when we harmonise any major scale.

Chord I - Major 7

Chord II - Minor 7

Chord III - Minor 7

Chord IV - Major 7

Chord V - Dominant 7 (7)

Chord VI - Minor 7

Chord VII - Minor 7b5

You will notice that chord I is always major 7, chord VI is always m7, chord II is always m7 and chord V is always 7.

This concept ties in with the chord qualities in the previous example.

In jazz, it is completely acceptable to change the *quality* of any chord (although you may wish to discuss this with the rest of the band first!). Let's change the quality of both chords I and VI to dominant 7.

The new chord progression is this:

Example 1f:

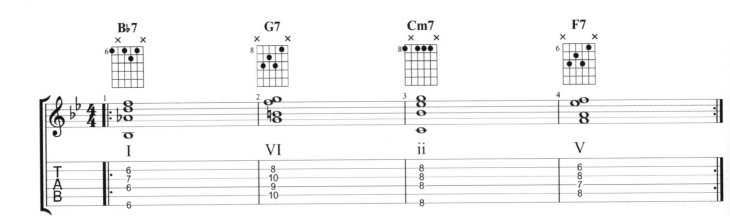

This new progression is a lot jazzier than the one in Example 1e.

Not only is this progression more bluesy, the fact that we are using dominant 7 chords gives us a much wider range of soloing options as we shall see in later chapters.

When we compare the standard 'B.B. King style', 12-bar blues with a jazz blues, we will see how the information in the previous few pages becomes relevant.

Standard 12-bar blues: (*Example 1a* repeated from earlier)

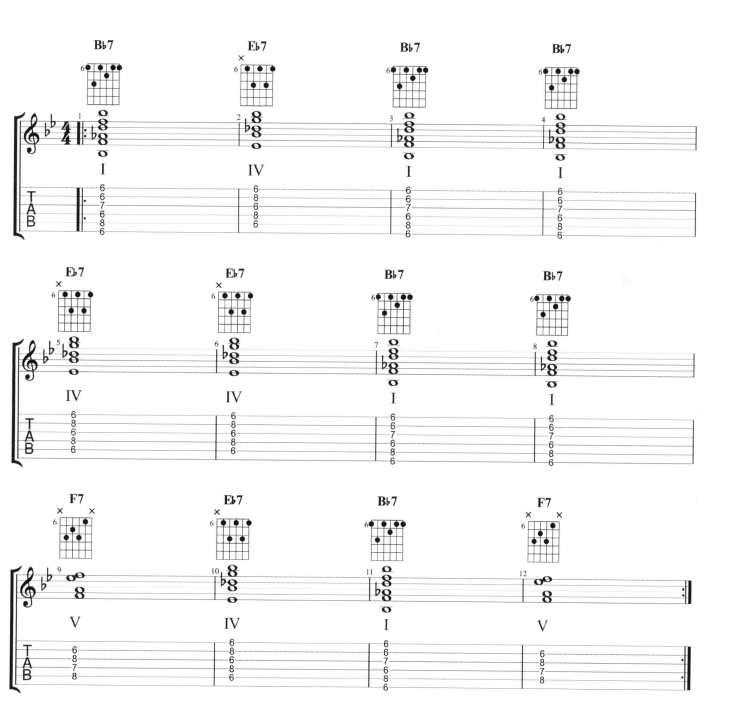

Example 1g *(12-bar Jazz Blues)*

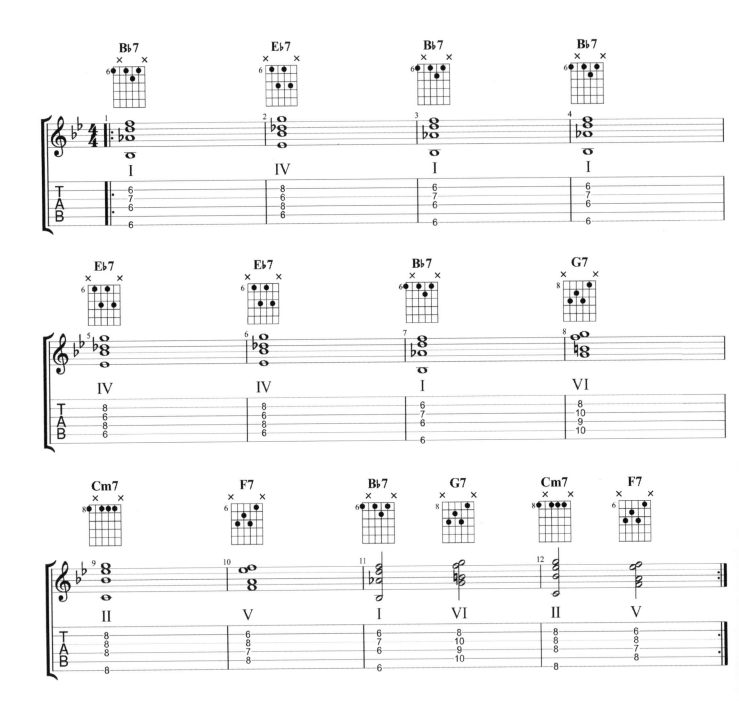

Focus on the Bb7 in bar 11 of the *top* (standard blues) example. Work *backwards* from this Bb7 and precede every chord by a dominant as we did in the previous pages. You should see how the extra chords in the jazz blues have arisen.

This four-bar section between bar 7 and bar 10 is referred to as the 'slow turnaround', as each chord lasts the duration of one bar.

You can see that the same sequence of chords occurs in the final two bars of the jazz blues. This is referred to as the quick turnaround, as the same chords are squeezed into just two bars. Although the quick turnaround happens in a shorter period, the method by which it was created is identical to the slow turnaround.

There are many other additions and alterations we can add to the jazz blues and we will examine them in detail in later chapters. For now, make sure you understand that;

1) Any chord can be preceded by a chord that is a perfect fifth away. The new chord is usually a dominant 7 or minor 7th chord.

2) Cycles of dominant chords can be built in this way. This is referred to as a cycle of fifths and is a common device in jazz.

3) It is acceptable to change the *quality* of any of these chords. It is most common to change the chord quality to become a dominant 7 chord. Changing the chord quality gives us new options for melodies and solos.

4) The I VI ii V turnaround in a jazz blues is created by building a cycle of fifths backwards from the tonic chord (in the above examples the tonic chord is Bb7).

5) The turnaround occurs in two places. The slow turnaround occurs between bars seven and ten and the quick turnaround occurs between bars eleven and twelve.

All the audio examples in this book are available for free from

www.fundamental-changes.com/audio-downloads

Chapter Two - Chord Voicings for the Jazz Blues

In this chapter, you will learn some common chord voicings used to play through the jazz blues in Bb.

The first method is to use *piano voicing* chords with roots on the 6th and 5th strings. These 'big' voicings are suitable to use when accompanying a vocalist or other melody instrument in a duo setting. Here are some basic voicings you should know.

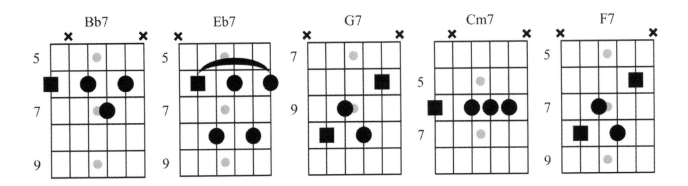

Try playing through the jazz blues chord chart using these voicings.

Example 2a:

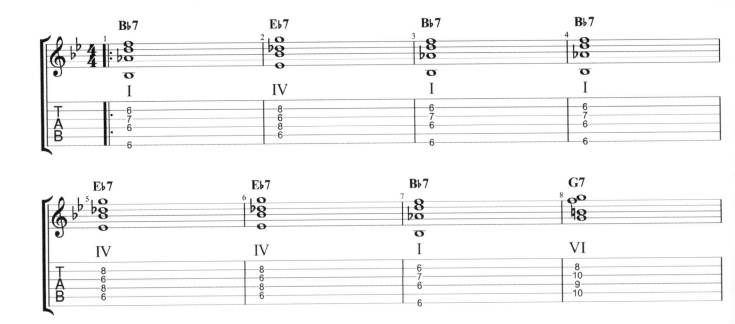

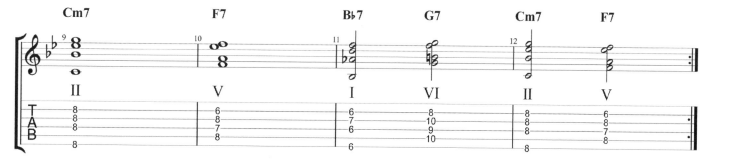

Next, we can use similar voicings, but add some extensions and alterations to the dominant chords that add a bit more of a jazz feel to the harmony.

Example 2b:

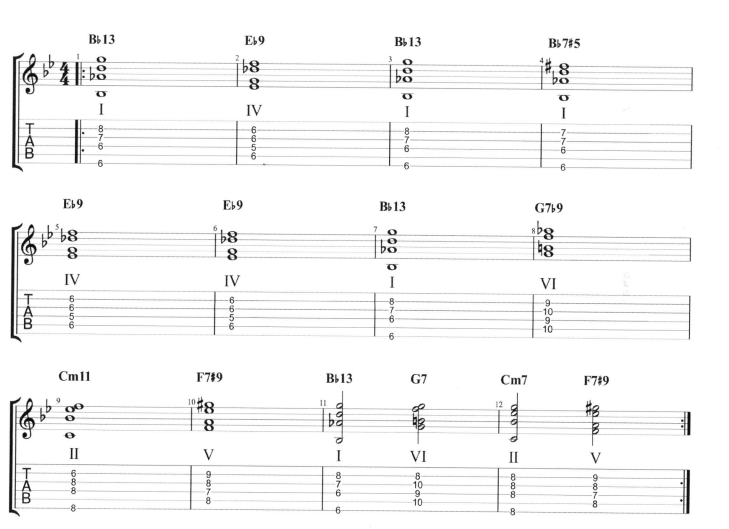

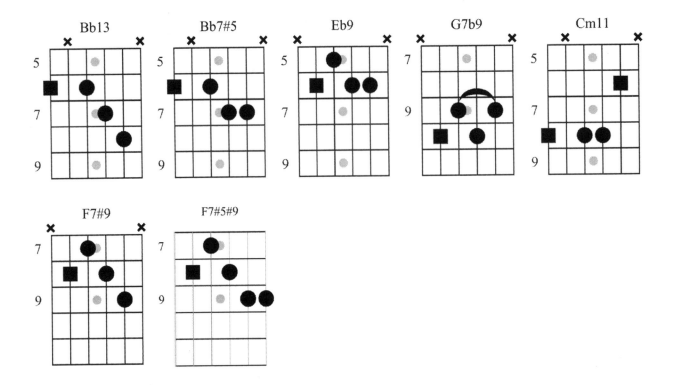

Finally, we will look at some drop 2 chords that are played only on the top four-strings. These voicings are great to use in a larger band setting. They give both the bass player and piano much more room to breath and avoid making the rhythm part too dense. I have combined some basic '7' chords with some extended and altered chords to add variation and colour.

You can hear the following drop 2 voicings demonstrated here.

Example 2c:

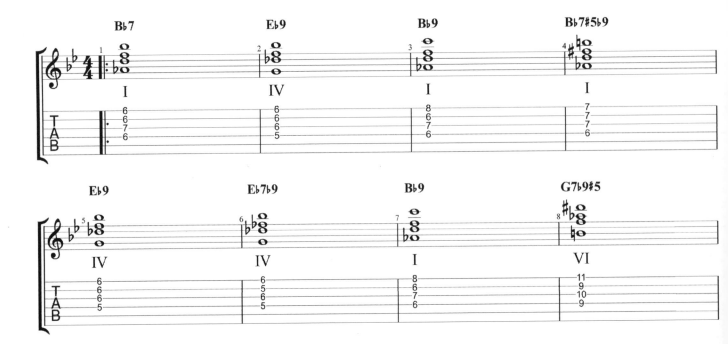

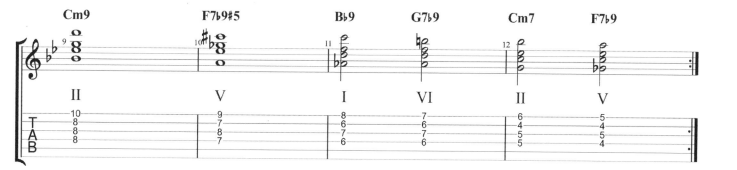

Here are the chord shapes you will need to play these changes on the top four-strings:

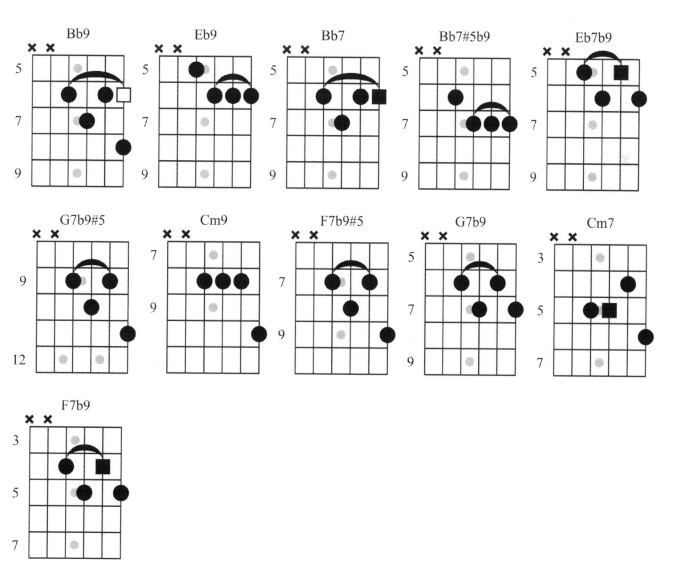

While these suggestions provide a good basis for comping through the changes in the jazz blues, they don't really come close to covering the many possibilities and options that are available for study. To learn a truly comprehensive approach to using all jazz guitar chords, check out my book **Jazz Guitar Chord Mastery**.

My intention in providing you with these chord charts and voicings is to allow you to hear from a harmonic viewpoint, how the jazz blues works and feels as a structure. I've not provided any specific rhythmic information in the charts so try to hear from the audio files how they could be played.

Chapter Three - Soloing on the First Seven Bars

The simplest way to approach soloing on a jazz blues is to split it into two sections. The jazz blues consists of a fairly static first seven bars moving between Bb7 and Eb7 (chords I and IV), and a harmonically 'busy' turnaround section in bars eight to twelve. By approaching these sections as separate entities, we can focus our practice to achieve the quickest, most articulate results.

As you may know, a '7th' chord is constructed by stacking four notes. The root of the chord, the 3rd, the 5th and the 7th.

The formulas of the chords are

Major 7th: 1 3 5 7

For example, BbMaj7 = Bb D F A

Dominant 7th: 1 3 5 b7

For example, Bb7 = Bb D F Ab

Minor 7th: 1 b3 5 b7

For example, Bbm7 = Bb Db F Ab

There is also the minor 7b5 chord. Its formula is 1 b3 b5 b7.

For example, Bbm7b5 = Bb Db Fb Ab.

It is not my intention to focus too much on theory in this book, so if you have questions about this section, please check out **The Practical Guide to Modern Music Theory for Guitarists.**

When we play the notes simultaneously we play a chord. When we play them one after another, we play an arpeggio.

If we play a Bb7 Arpeggio over a Bb7 chord, it will always fit and sound good because it contains all the notes of the chord.

Playing appropriate arpeggios over chords is one of the most important elements of jazz soloing so we will begin by learning the Bb7 arpeggio.

The numbers in the arpeggio diagram below show the intervals of the chord.

R = Root

^3 = Major 3rd

b3 = Minor 3rd

p5 = Perfect (natural) 5th

b7 = b7 (pronounced 'flat 7')

Example 3a:

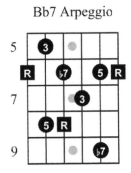

Learn to play this arpeggio ascending and descending. Practice each new arpeggio with a metronome set on 40 bpm and play one note per click.

When you can play this arpeggio at 80 bpm, *half* the metronome speed back down to 40bpm and play two notes per beat (1/8th notes). You can gradually increase the metronome speed once more. 120 bpm is a good goal, but remember, this book is not about technique or speed. For now, your only goal is to make sure the arpeggio is memorised.

Now we can take a look at the Eb7 arpeggio:

Example 3b:

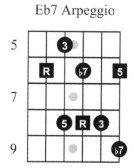

Eb7 Arpeggio

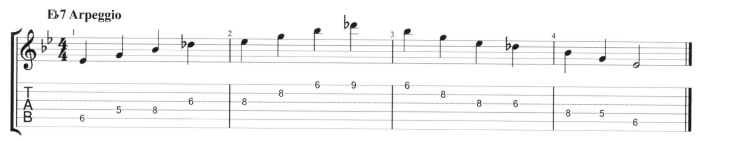

Eb7 Arpeggio

Repeat the process to learn the Eb7. Don't move on until you can play both arpeggios from memory, backwards and forwards.

The following exercises will help you master the important and common change from Bb7 to Eb7 using arpeggios. This change occurs in many jazz standards, not just the jazz blues.

Begin by playing five notes up through each arpeggio, and then resting for a bar. Always begin from the lowest root of each chord.

Example 3c:

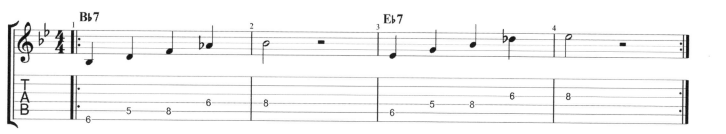

The following repeating chord sequence is included on *backing track one*:

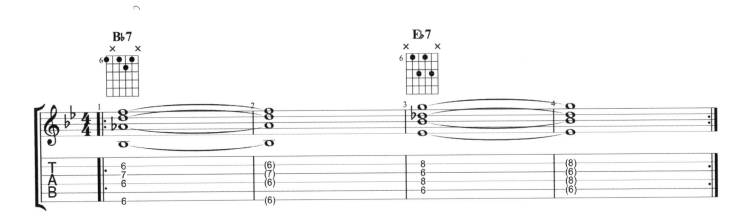

Now reverse the pattern so you're starting from the higher root and descending through the arpeggio.

Example 3d:

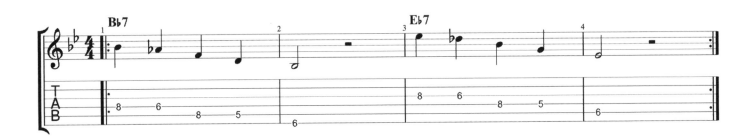

Next, instead of beginning from the root of each arpeggio, repeat the process ascending and descending from the *3rds* of each arpeggio (this is the second note in each arpeggio).

Example 3e:

Example 3f:

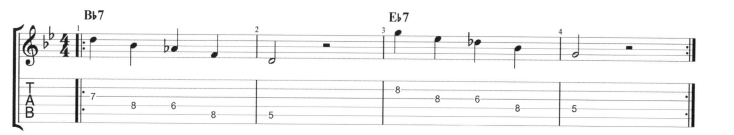

Now practice ascending and descending from the 5ths of each arpeggio:

Example 3g:

(Only the ascending figure is shown due to space constraints)

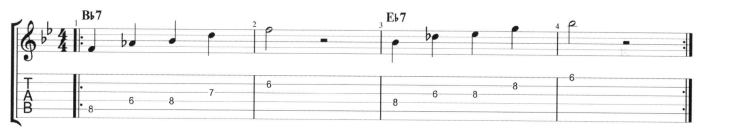

Finally, ascend and descend from the b7s of each arpeggio.

Example 3h:

The next stage is to learn to join the two arpeggios together as you would when you are soloing. To do this, begin by reducing the length of time you have to play on each chord to one bar.

Backing track two cycles the following chord progression:

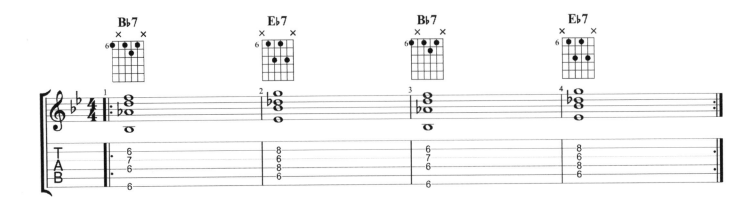

Because we have less time on each chord, it means we need to think faster, and therefore we internalise the sound and shape of each arpeggio much more deeply than before.

We will play four arpeggio notes up each scale as we did earlier, however this time there will be no rest and we must jump immediately to the correct arpeggio note on the following chord.

If this is too tricky to begin with, try just playing three notes and resting on beat four, but try to work up to playing four notes per bar as soon as possible.

Example 3i:

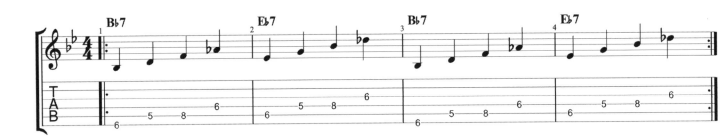

Practice this exercise beginning on the root, 3rd, 5th and b7th of each chord. Practice each one ascending and descending. This is a important stage so don't miss it out. I have not included the notation for reasons of space, but the information in exercises 3c - 3h should help you out if you get stuck.

There are opportunities to play each interval in different octaves. For example, the previous exercise could also be played up an octave like this:

Example 3j:

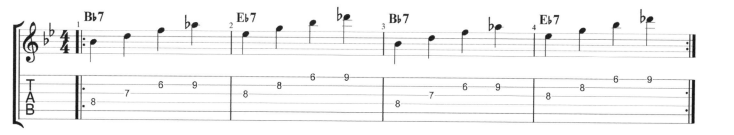

If you run out of available notes in this position, simply double back on yourself, rather than reaching up the neck into a new position.

These exercises are extremely important in building up your confidence with the arpeggio shapes and your ability to play any specific interval you chose. You will see why this is so important in Chapter Five.

Once you can change between arpeggios as the chord changes instantly, it is time to 'join up the dots' to create a smooth transition between arpeggios. This is the foundation on which all good jazz guitar solos are built.

Chapter Four - Smooth Transitions between Arpeggios

In this chapter you will continue to develop your melodic fluency and aural skills by focusing on moving smoothly between the arpeggios of Bb7 and Eb7 in small areas of the fretboard.

In this section we will move to *the closest note* in the new arpeggio when the chord changes. This process helps highlight these harmonic movements in our solos and *articulates* the chord changes as they happen. In this way, we can choose to let melodies and solos mirror the harmony provided by the rhythm section. This melodic articulation is one of the most defining characteristics of jazz.

Let's begin by looking at the transitions that are possible when moving from the Bb7 arpeggio to the Eb7 arpeggio, focusing on just the top two strings.

Study the following diagrams:

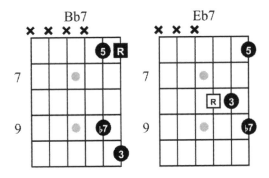

In both diagrams, the note Bb remains in the same place (it is the root of the Bb7 arpeggio and the 5th of the Eb7 arpeggio).

However, on the second string, the b7 of Bb7 (Ab) falls by a semitone to become the 3rd of Eb7 (G).

The 3rd of Bb7 (D), falls by a semitone to become the b7 of the Eb7 arpeggio (Db).

These movements are extremely strong melodic elements and sound great when highlighted in a jazz solo. It is essential to find these types of close movements to articulate the chord changes in any jazz standard.

Using backing track two (one bar per chord), play four arpeggio notes per bar, and as the chord changes, *target* the closest note in the next arpeggio.

The following examples will get you started. Remember, you are only allowed to play on the top two strings of the guitar (for now!).

Example 4a:

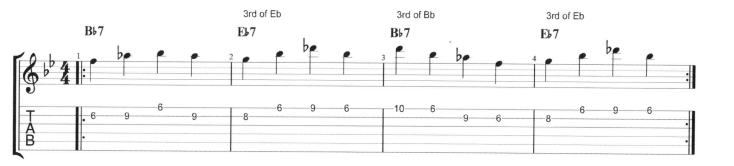

Example 4b:

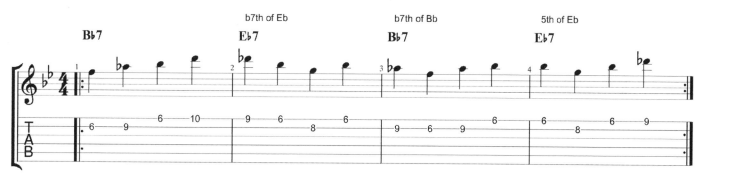

These two examples only demonstrate this exercise for four bars, but you should keep playing the arpeggios and linking the shapes smoothly for as long as you can. You will quickly begin to find these exercises repetitive; this is a good thing. You are starting to memorise the points where you can articulately change between the two chords.

These exercises are essential, because they provide the foundation for everything you will learn about melodic jazz soloing. They also train your ears, your fretboard fluency and your muscle memory, so when we are dealing with more complex concepts like chromatic approach notes and altered scales, you can always resolve any melodic idea to a strong chord tone.

When you feel you have exhausted all the possibilities with this two-string group, move on and repeat the exercise with the arpeggio notes on the second and third strings.

Begin by observing the potential changes on paper, then target them in your playing. There are many opportunities to link the arpeggios together on the third string.

Here are the arpeggio diagrams to get you started.

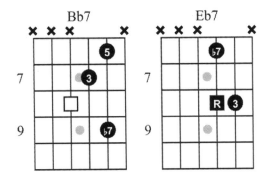

Gradually move the two-string groupings across the fretboard until you have worked on the fifth and sixth strings. The notes of the Eb7 arpeggio were not included in the earlier diagram, so here is a diagram of the full arpeggios for both chords.

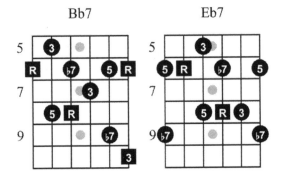

When you have practiced this exercise with two-string groups, move on to working with three-string groups.

Continue to play four notes per bar, but this time allow yourself to work with arpeggios on three strings. If you have practiced the ideas in the previous examples thoroughly, working with three strings shouldn't be too difficult. At any time, feel free to go back to working with two-string groups if you have any gaps in your knowledge.

Here are the arpeggio shapes isolated on the top three-strings, followed by some possible 'routes' to help you get started.

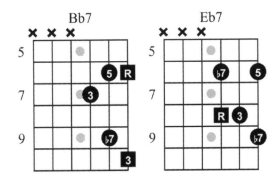

Example 4c:

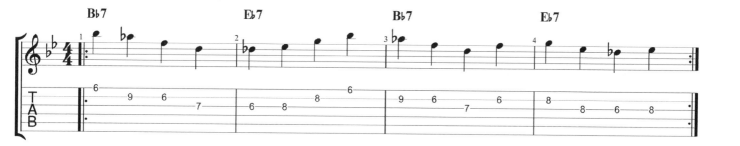

Example 4d:

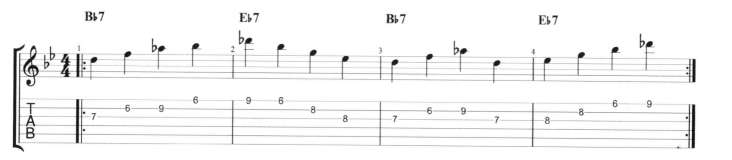

Next, start working with four-string and five-string groups, before joining the arpeggios together over all six strings.

Be observant when you practice. If you notice any area of the neck you're avoiding, go back and focus on just two or three-string groups until you're confident. Remember to isolate the bass strings of the guitar too.

Chapter Five - Targeting Specific Intervals

We have looked at the guitar neck in terms of joining 'shapes' when soloing, but it is also important to learn to view the neck in terms of the actual *intervals* that you are playing at any given time. This will help enormously later when it comes to targeting arpeggio notes when we look at more complex ideas such as chromatic approach note patterns and scale choices in chapters six and seven.

The idea is to target specific intervals of each chord and see how they move as the chords change.

The following exercises are vital for mastering your fretboard.

We will begin by only playing the root of each arpeggio over the chord changes. Be patient if this seems simple, as the following exercises build towards complete mastery quickly.

Exercise one - play only the root of each chord.

Example 5a:

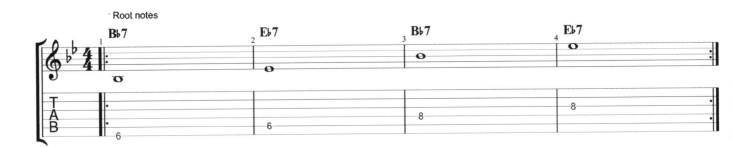

Notice that in this position, there is more than one root in each shape. Keep playing over backing track two until you are confident you can find the root of each arpeggio in any octave.

Now isolate the 3rd of each arpeggio. This is more difficult than playing the root and will increase your vision and aural skills while soloing.

Exercise two - play only the 3rd of each arpeggio.

Example 5b:

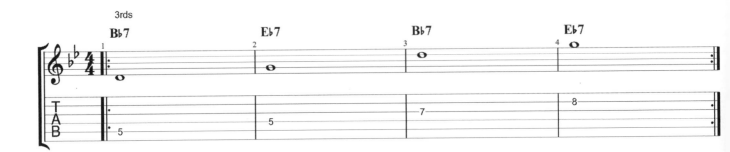

Once again, there are 3rds in different octaves, and not all of them are included in the previous example.

Repeat this exercise for the 5ths and b7s of each arpeggio. Use the diagrams in Chapter Three to help you.

Now let's make this exercise a bit more musical. Play the 3rd of the Bb7 chord in any octave, and then move to the closest note in the Eb7 arpeggio.

We begin on the 3rd of Bb7 and look for specific, targeted movements between the Bb7 and Eb7 arpeggios.

The 3rd of the Bb7 arpeggio (D), can either resolve down to the b7 of the Eb7 arpeggio (Db), or up to the root of the Eb7 arpeggio (Eb).

Example 5c:

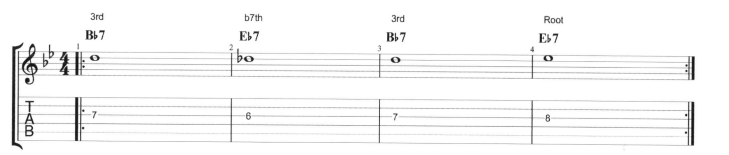

In jazz, the movement from the 3rd of one chord and the 7th of another, is one the strongest resolutions possible. While the 3rd of Bb7 (D) *can* move up to the root of Eb (Eb), I recommend that you spend some time learning to hear the resolution from the 3rd to the b7. This is called *guide tone* movement.

Repeat the previous exercise beginning on both the 5ths and b7s of the Bb7 chord. You will notice that the 5th of Bb can either rise one tone to become the 3rd of Eb, or descend to become the root.

Take particular notice of the movement from the b7 of Bb (Ab) as it falls by a semitone to become the 3rd of the Eb chord (G).

Example 5d:

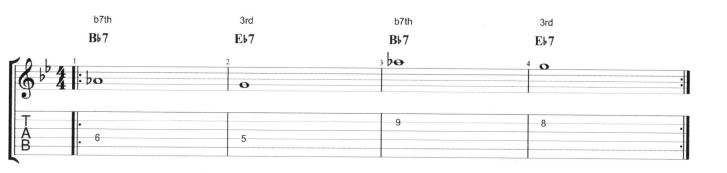

It may seem like you are doing a great deal of 'prep work' before actually soloing and building jazz blues lines, but you will quickly hear the benefit of this groundwork reflected by the strength of your jazz lines.

You should be able to hear how strong the guide tone movement is between the 3rds and 7ths of the chords. Let's combine them to make a simple solo that articulates the chord changes. Using only the 3rd and b7 of each chord, combine them in all octaves making sure you always move a semitone as the chord changes.

Here is one possible way to solo using guide tones over the changes:

Example 5e:

Notice how I begin the exercise simply, with just two notes per bar, and gradually move to slightly more complex rhythms. Feel free to move into 1/8th notes as you gain confidence, but don't lose sight of the fundamental point of this exercise; to hear guide tone movements and play them accurately over changes.

You can check to see if you're doing this exercise correctly by playing it without a backing track. If you are changing chords in the right place and hitting either a 3rd or b7 on the change you will be able to hear the chords changing in your head as you solo. The ability to imply a chord change by the choice of notes in a solo, is another fundamental element to great jazz guitar soloing.

Try playing a solo based around the Bb Minor Pentatonic / Blues scale, but add in the guide tone movements from the previous examples to articulate the chord changes. You will find that by combining the Minor Pentatonic / Blues scale with these concepts, you go a long way towards playing a strong jazz blues solo. Stay away from bending notes and vibrato and stick to 1/4 note, and 1/8th note rhythms.

Here is the scale diagram for the Bb Minor Blues scale, and a couple of sample licks that combine the blues scale with guide tone and arpeggio-based voice leading.

Bb Blues Scale

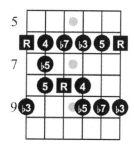

Example 5f:

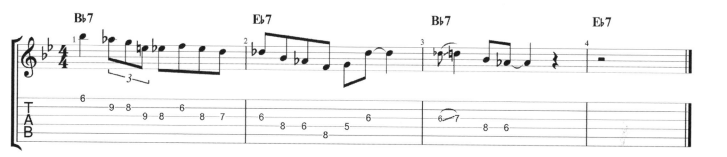

Example 5g:

It is worth spending time here finding ways to navigate the I - IV change using the minor blues scale and the related arpeggios to target guide tones. There are, however, other scales and approaches that can be used to sound more 'jazzy'.

In the next chapter, we will study the Mixolydian 'Bebop' scale, and learn how it combines with arpeggio ideas to create a traditional jazz sound.

Chapter Six - Using the Mixolydian Bebop Scale

The Mixolydian Bebop scale (or just 'The Bebop' scale), is the most important, and common scale choice for soloing over a *static* dominant 7 chord. A static dominant 7 chord is one which can be played indefinitely, and does not need to resolve to a I chord. The opposite of a static dominant chord is a *functional* dominant chord, which will normally be part of a ii V I progression and wants to *resolve* to another chord. A functional dominant chord is a point of tension in a chord progression, and this will be discussed in Chapter Eleven.

Both chords I and IV of the jazz blues progression (Bb7 and Eb7) are normally treated as static dominants.

The Mixolydian mode is the fifth mode of the major scale and has the scale formula **1** 2 **3** 4 **5** 6 **b7**

As you can see, it contains all of the notes from the dominant 7 arpeggio (1, 3, 5 and b7), plus some other notes too. All the other notes generally sound great on a blues.

A quick theory side note: The scale degrees 2, 4 and 6 when played in conjunction with a '7th' chord are normally given the names 9, 11 and 13.

To clarify this, look at the following scale formula:

1 2 **3** 4 **5** 6 **b7 (8/1)** 9 **3** 11 **5** 13 **b7**

In the higher octave, the chord tones keep the same names (1, 3, 5, b7), and the extensions are named 9, 11 and 13.

In the scale of Bb Mixolydian, (Bb C D Eb F G Ab), the arpeggios notes are Bb, D, F, and Ab.

The note C is the 9th, Eb is the 11th and G is the 13th.

There is, however, one small problem with the Mixolydian mode because jazz players like to do two important things:

1) Play in 1/8th notes

2) Normally keep arpeggio tones on the beat

Study the following.

Example 6a:

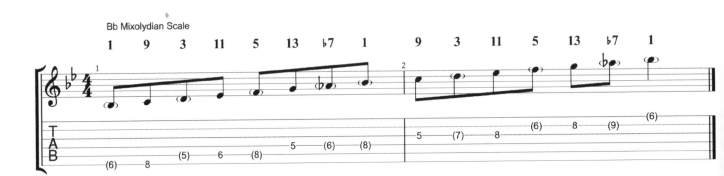

Pay careful attention to which intervals fall on the beat in bars one and two. The arpeggio tones are bracketed, and in the first bar you can see that everything works well; the arpeggio notes fall nicely on the beat until we return to the root. The root note falls on the off-beat of beat four. This means that in the higher octave, all the 'wrong' notes are falling on the beats. I.e., the 9th, 11th and 13th now fall on the beats, and the arpeggio notes fall between the beats. This is because the scale contains seven notes.

Playing arpeggio tones continuously on off beats creates weak, inarticulate solos.

Jazz musicians solve this problem by inserting a *chromatic passing note* between the b7 and the root, as it is the lack of a note between the b7 and root that messes up the pattern in the first place.

By adding in this *natural 7th* between the b7 and the root, we create an eight-note scale that always works well when played with 1/8th or 1/16th notes. This is shown below.

Example 6b:

As you can see, by inserting a *chromatic passing note* between the b7 and the root at the end of bar one, the strong arpeggio notes remain on the beat into bar two.

What's more, when you solo using the Bebop scale in 1/8th notes, If you you begin your line with an arpeggio note on a strong beat of the bar and play stepwise scale ideas, you automatically keep the strong arpeggio notes on the beat, whichever direction you play in. The weaker extensions will always fall on the off-beats.

You can see why jazz musicians love using Bebop scales!

These are the diagrams for the Bb Bebop and Eb Bebop scales. The added chromatic natural 7ths are shown by a hollow circle:

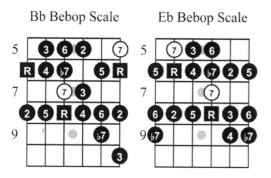

We will first focus on how to use the Bb Bebop scale. Everything in this section is immediately transferable to the Eb Bebop scale.

First, make sure you have memorised the Bb Bebop scale and can play it in 1/8th notes ascending and descending at 120 bpm. Play it over *backing track three*, a static Bb7 vamp, and listen to how the chord tones always fall on the beat, when you begin with an arpeggio note on the beat and play in 1/8th notes.

When you are confident, move back to *backing track two* and practice the following exercise.

Begin on the root of the Bb7 chord and ascend eight notes through the Bb Bebop scale. Play a final ninth note that targets the closest note in the Eb7 arpeggio, just as you learned in Chapter Four.

Example 6c:

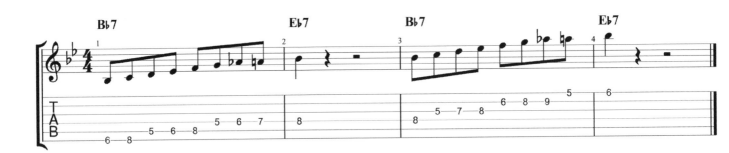

We can also try this idea descending from the roots.

Example 6d:

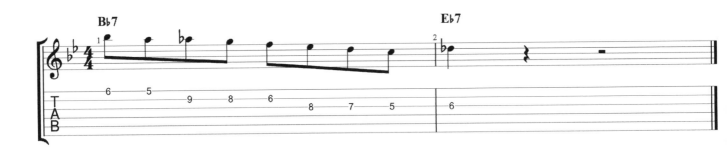

Notice that in this example, I double back and target the b7 of the Eb, although I could have equally continued descending into the 5th (Bb) of the Eb7 chord. Given the choice, I normally target a b7 as it is a strong-sounding guide tone.

Practice descending the Bb Bebop scale from the higher octave root.

Now ascend and descend from the 3rds of the Bb7 chord:

Example 6e:

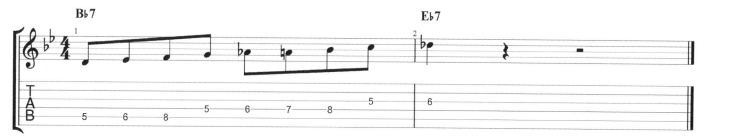

Example 6f:

In Example 6f, I gave two possible points of resolution, to the b7 of Eb. However, you could opt to repeat the final note and resolve to the root of the Eb7 chord.

Practice ascending and descending the Bb Bebop scale from the 3rds of Bb7 in every available octave in this position. Find all the possible ways you can resolve to the Eb7 chord on beat one of bar two.

Now work on the same ideas, but ascend from both the 5th and the b7 of the Bb Bebop scale. Always resolve to an arpeggio tone of Eb7.

Next, repeat the process, with the Eb Bebop scale over the Eb7 chord and resolve to a chord tone of Bb7.

First make sure you have memorised the Eb Mixolydian Bebop scale:

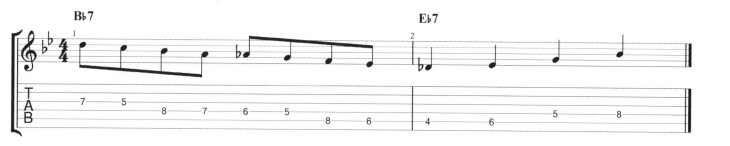

Use *backing track two* and don't play anything in the first bar. You can hear this demonstrated ascending and descending from the root.

Example 6g:

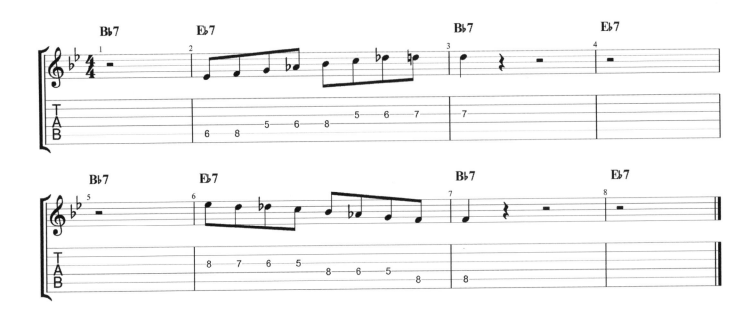

As you can see, when you ascend or descend the Eb7 Bebop scale from the root of the Eb7 chord the resolution can be a little clunky. We will fix this in Chapter Seven when we study chromatic passing notes.

Continue exploring the Eb Bebop scale by playing eight notes ascending or descending from all the available 3rds, 5ths and b7s of the Eb7 chord. Always resolve the ninth note to a chord tone of Bb7, even if it means repeating the final note twice. The following examples show some possible alternatives, beginning from the 3rd, 5th and b7 of the Eb7 chord.

Example 6h: Descend from the 3rd of Eb7

Example 6i: Descend from the 5th of Eb7

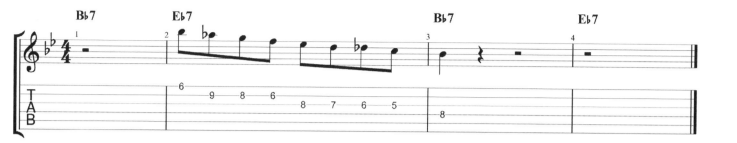

Example 6j: Ascend from the b7 of Eb7

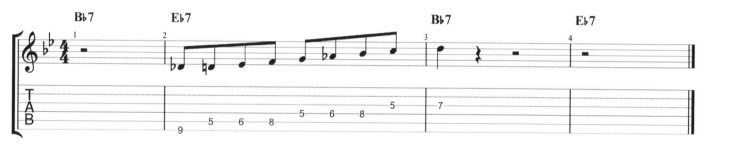

Exhausting all the possible resolutions may take some time but be patient and go slowly because understanding how to resolve a Bebop scale run at any point in the scale is an essential waypoint on your journey.

The next stage is to join the Bb and Eb Bebop scales together by continuing a scale run *over* the chord change.

Look at the following line. It begins on the Bb Bebop scale and changes to the Eb Bebop scale after targeting a chord tone on beat one of bar two.

Example 6k:

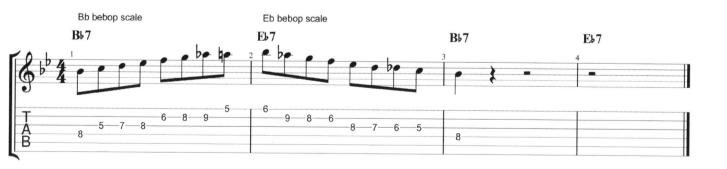

Here is another idea beginning from the 3rd of the Bb7 chord.

Example 6l:

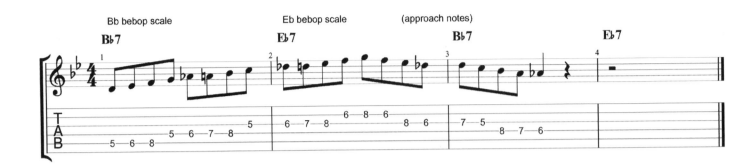

The second bar of Example 6l is interesting because instead of running straight down the Eb Bebop scale, I use an *approach note pattern* to target the 3rd of the Bb7 chord in bar three.

Make sure you hit an arpeggio tone of the new chord on beat one of the new bar. If you must change the order of the final few notes of the preceding bar to achieve this, that's fine.

This concept gets much more elaborate and musical in Chapter Seven. For now, make sure you are aiming for those chord tones.

You don't have to begin your blues line on the first beat of the bar. The following examples begin from beats two, three and four of the Bb7 bar:

Example 6m:

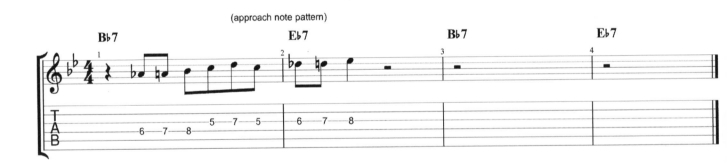

Example 6n:

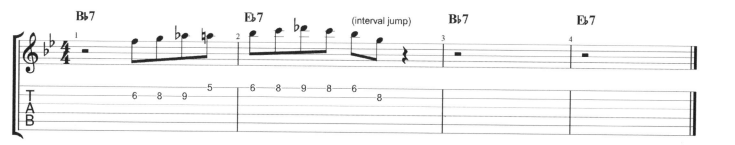

Example 6o:

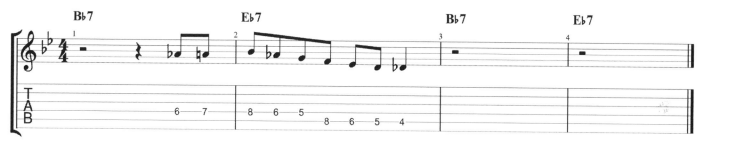

Don't worry about the interval skips and approach note patterns in the previous examples. Later you'll learn many melodic devices to help the arpeggio notes fall on the beat.

If you want to put a non-chord tone (9th, 11th or 13th), on beat one, there is always a way to resolve this tension with a chromatic passing note back to an arpeggio tone on beat two. You will find this often happens when you begin on beat four of bar one.

Another great way to practice is to set a task of practicing with phrases of a specific length. Try playing 4-, 6-, 8-, or 10-note lines; you will quickly learn how these set phrase-lengths sound. You could try 8-note phrases beginning from beat two, three or four, or maybe 6-note phrases beginning on beats three and four.

Make sure your lines cross the bar line so you are forced to practice hitting the changes and placing a chord tone on the beat.

You should now hear that bebop scales, combined with hitting arpeggio tones on chord changes, form a large part of jazz vocabulary. When we add in chromatic passing notes and approach note patterns, we really start to get to grips with the fundamental principles of bebop guitar language.

Chromaticism is an essential melodic element of jazz music and is discussed in the following chapter.

Chapter Seven - Chromatic Passing Notes

In the previous chapter, we examined the Mixolydian Bebop scale, and saw that it is formed by adding a chromatic passing note between the b7 and root of the scale. This eight-note scale functions well in jazz, because any 1/8th note line beginning from a chord tone will 'automatically' place a chord tone on the beat.

However, as we also saw in the previous chapter, this concept can fall apart when we solo over a chord change or get more adventurous with the melody. For example…

Example 7a:

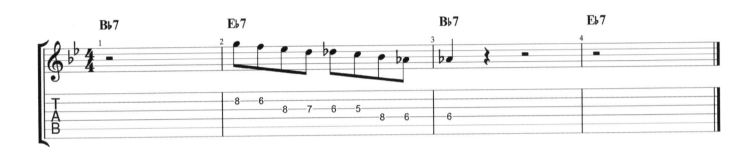

Descending the Eb Bebop scale from the 3rd leads to a situation where the final note of the Eb bar is a chord tone of the Bb7 chord in the following bar. While this is by no means incorrect, we can create a much smoother line by adding a *chromatic* note between beat four and beat one. A chromatic note is *any* note that does not lie in the scale.

Examine how I change the previous example to create a smoother melody line.

Example 7b:

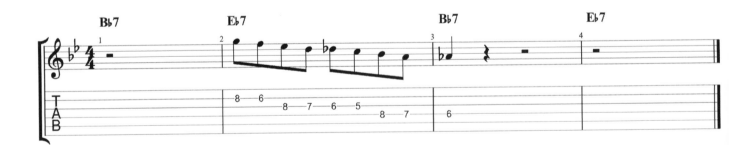

The new note on the final beat of bar two (A), is a *chromatic passing note* between the Bb on beat four and the Ab on beat one. As it falls on an off-beat (*between* the beats), it is not felt as a strong dissonance. In fact, it makes for a smoother melodic transition between the two chords.

A chromatic passing note can be added any time you are a tone away from a target note when on beat four.

Example 7c shows another example that moves from Bb7 to Eb7.

Example 7c:

Again, study what happens in beat four. In this example, I pass from the 5th of the Bb7 chord (F), to the 3rd of the Eb7 chord via a chromatic approach note. Again, the chromatic approach note falls on the off-beat of beat four.

In the next example, I move chromatically from the 5th of the Bb7 chord, to the root of the Eb7 chord before continuing the line with a bebop scale and arpeggio idea.

Example 7d:

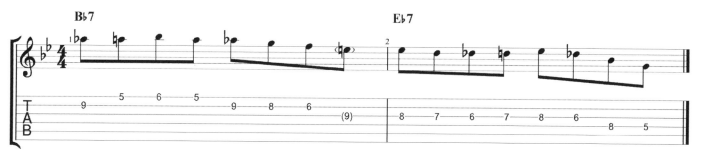

Chromatic passing notes are used all the time in jazz. Anytime you are a tone away from a target note, you can fill in the gap with a chromatic passing note.

Another useful way to use chromatic notes is when we are a semitone away from our desired target note on beat four. For example, let's imagine I want my melodic solo to move from the b7 on beat four of the Bb7 chord to the 3rd of the Eb7 chord on beat one.

I am already one semitone away from the note I wish to target, so I cannot insert a chromatic note between the two melody notes. Instead, I can use an *enclosure* and play a chromatic note the other side of the target note.

Example 7e:

This enclosure is just one of many common *approach note patterns* that are used in jazz. Here is a longer bebop line that incorporates the previous concept:

Example 7f:

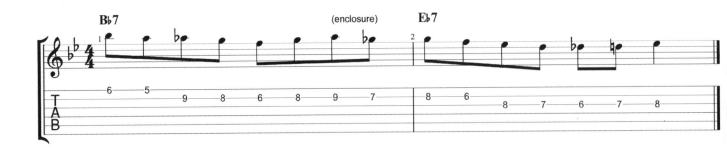

Can you hear how using a chromatic approach note to immediately precede the chord tone in Eb7 adds real strength and interest to the line?

Enclosures don't necessarily have to use a chromatic note. Sometimes we use an enclosure that uses notes from the scale.

Example 7g:

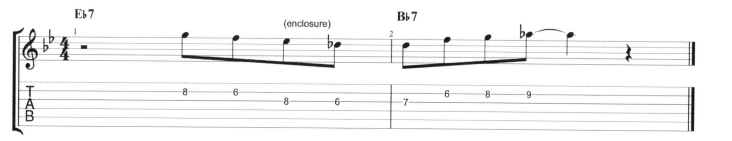

The previous line targets the 3rd of Bb7 (D) with an enclosure. It just so happens that both the enclosure notes are in the Eb Mixolydian Bebop scale.

Example 7h is a line moving from Bb7 to Eb7 which uses an enclosure to target the 3rd of Eb7.

Example 7h:

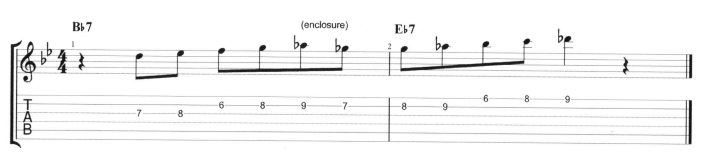

The next line uses an enclosure to target the b7 of Eb7.

Example 7i:

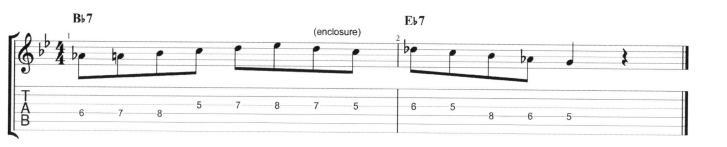

Another use of chromatic passing notes is between a non-arpeggio note (extension) and an arpeggio tone of the same chord.

Until now, we have always played an arpeggio tone on each beat of the bar. This is an essential part of learning to play and hear jazz music, but as you progress you will find that your ears often want to place a non-arpeggio note on the beat.

We can always use a chromatic note to move from a non-arpeggio tone to an arpeggio tone.

Study the following line that moves from Eb7 to Bb7. When the chord changes to Bb7 I deliberately place the 13th of Bb7 (G) on the beat.

Do you see how I use a chromatic passing note on the off-beat of beat one to get back to an arpeggio note (the 5th, F) on beat two?

Example 7j:

I could have also used an enclosure to target the b7 of Bb7. Here's the same line with a different ending.

Example 7k:

This kind of chromaticism may take a little getting used to, but as long at the chromatic note is played on an off-beat it will always work.

The same approach can be used when moving from the 9th to the root.

Example 7l:

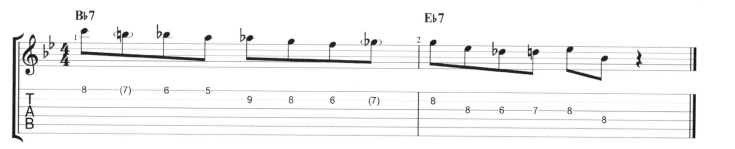

Jazz lines can quickly become chromatic and interesting by simply combining target notes with the Bebop scale, chromatic passing notes and enclosures.

A chromatic passing note can also be used between the 11th of the scale and the 5th, but placing the 11th of a major or dominant chord on the beat has to be handled with care.

If the 11th (4th) of a major chord is played on the beat it creates a semitone clash with the major 3rd in the chord. For the moment, I'd suggest avoiding it.

We will look at more detailed practice ideas in the following chapter when we look at approach note patterns. For now, one way to practice is to turn off your metronome and imagine you are playing the final two beats of one bar, and the first beat of the next.

Play three notes of the Bebop scale (beginning from a chord tone), and try to find a chromatic passing note or enclosure to play on the final note of the bar that targets a chord tone of the next chord.

Examples 7m-7o show you how.

Example 7m:

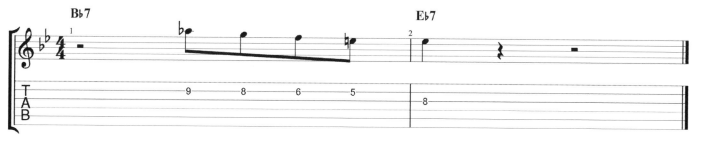

Example 7n:

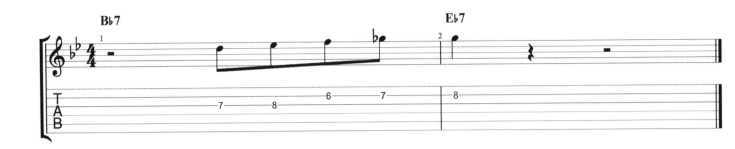

Example 7o:

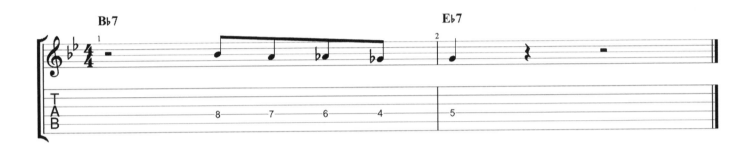

Try to be methodical, and don't worry about using a metronome at first. Treat this as a bit of exploration.

All these short chromatic ideas quickly get into your ears, and you will create some excellent, articulate chromatic licks over beautiful chord changes.

Chapter Eight - Chromatic Approach Note Patterns

Chapters Six and Seven discussed approaches to blues soloing using the Mixolydian Bebop scale and chromatic approach notes, however, jazz language is primarily derived from arpeggios and 'decorations' to those arpeggios.

Remember the basic principle of jazz soloing: keep arpeggio tones on the beat, and non-arpeggio tones off the beat. If we consider what we learned in the previous chapter about chromatic passing notes, it is reasonable to suggest that we can place any chromatic note on an off-beat, as long as it resolves to an arpeggio tone on the beat.

This concept is the starting point to explore some common decorations to arpeggio based soloing.

Let's refresh the Bb7 arpeggio:

Bb7 Arpeggio

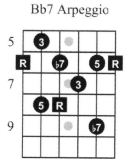

We will start by adding a chromatic approach note a semitone below each of the arpeggio tones of Bb7. Each chromatic note will be one semitone below the target note and played on an off-beat.

In the following diagram, the target notes of the Bb7 arpeggio are solid, and the chromatic approach notes are hollow. Learn these ideas without a metronome at first.

Example 8a:

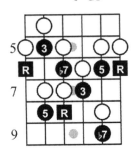

Bb7 Arpeggio

When you get confident, play the previous exercise as a continuous line.

Example 8b:

Also learn this idea descending.

Example 8c:

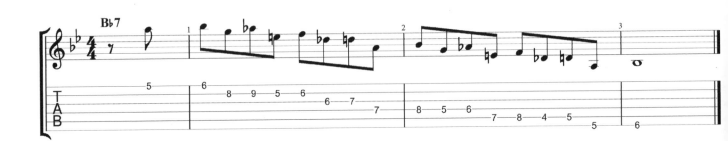

Now apply the same idea to the Eb7 arpeggio. To save space I've written the following examples as 1/8th notes, but don't be afraid to add lots of space between each note pair so you can internalise this sound more easily.

This technique can be applied to any arpeggio, so proceed slowly and learn the sound carefully and fluently.

Example 8d:

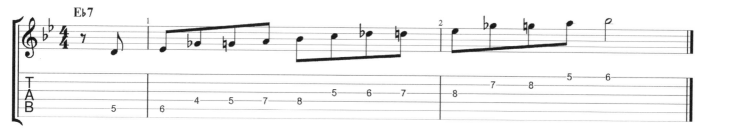

Example 8e:

When I first learnt these concepts, the main difficulty I had was using them musically.

I finally realised that they work best combined with the voice leading over chord changes ideas we examined in Chapter Seven. They can be used at any time as an approach into a target note of a new chord.

These patterns are useful and distinctive when played over static chords. I highly recommend getting used to their sound and rhythmic placement over one-chord vamps such as backing tracks three and four.

The following lines demonstrate the use of the 'semitone below' approach note pattern.

Example 8f:

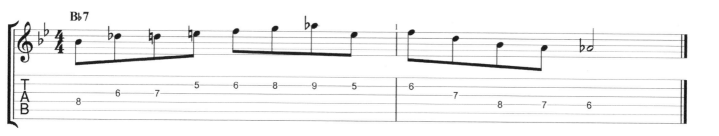

Example 8g:

There are other chromatic approach note patterns that are used, but next most important one is the *semitone below / scale step above* pattern.

As its name suggests, this pattern starts in a similar manner to the semitone below pattern, but we add in another note, this time from the scale appropriate to the chord (in this case, the Mixolydian mode)

This pattern allows us to put a chromatic tone *on the beat,* and it will sound fantastic, as long as you resolve it correctly.

Example 8h shows you how to play the *semitone below / scale step above* pattern on the root of the Bb7 arpeggio.

Example 8h*:*

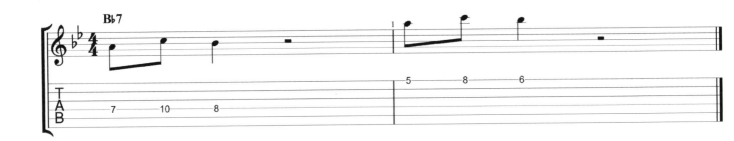

As you can see, the chromatic note is now placed on the beat.

Here are the arpeggio tones of the Bb7 chord played with the same pattern. Notice that for *all* the tones, except for the 3rd, the scale step is always one tone above the target note.

Example 8i:

Don't worry about playing these patterns with a metronome or backing track at first. It is more important to learn them slowly and accurately. They're a great way to test how well you *really* know these arpeggios, because you must visualise and hear the target note far in advance of playing it.

When you are getting to grips with this pattern, play through the whole arpeggio, targeting one arpeggio note per bar over backing track three. It should sound something like this.

Example 8j:

Gradually increase the frequency of the approach note patterns, and experiment with the rhythms too. Repeat this process descending, and for the Eb7 arpeggio shown below with *backing track four.*

Example 8k:

Try skipping intervals within the arpeggio too. For example, first target the root, then the 5th, then the 3rd and finally the b7th. Try any combination you can think of!

The biggest challenge is to bring these approach note patterns into your actual soloing, and combine them with the other fundamental jazz concepts in this book. This is a long term goal, but by simply practicing these approach note patterns every day, your ears will gradually bring them into your playing.

The following lines combine all the different concepts covered so far in this book. They consist of arpeggios, Bebop scales, target notes, chromatic passing notes and approach note patterns.

Lines moving from Bb7 to Eb7

Example 8l:

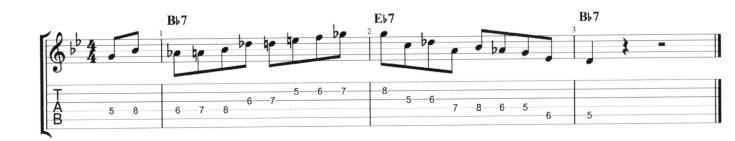

Example 8m:

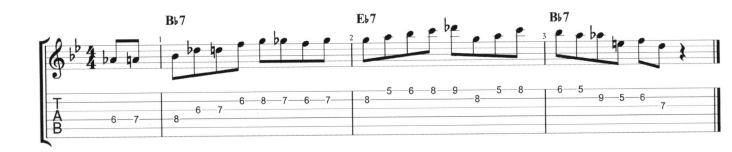

Example 8n:

Example 8o:

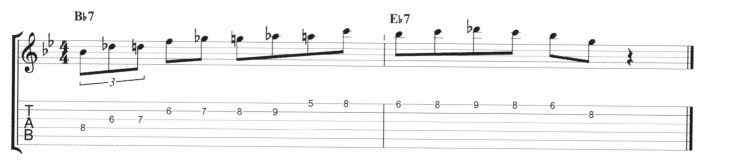

Lines moving from Bb7 to Eb7

Example 8p:

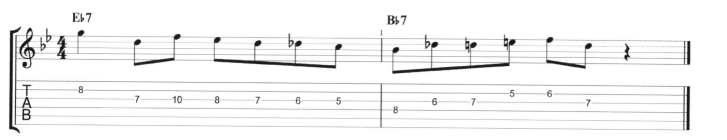

Example 8q:

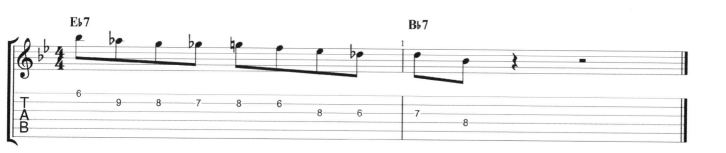

When you are learning these licks, analyse them and discover how they are constructed. By reverse engineering them, you will discover a great deal about how the concepts in the previous chapters are used musically.

To begin with, practice each line slowly without a metronome, but as soon as you are able to, play them with a click or backing track so you can hear how the strong notes of the chord still normally fall on the beat.

Chapter Nine - Adding the bV Diminished 7 Chord

A common addition to the jazz blues is the inclusion of a diminished 7 chord, built on the bV (b5) degree of the tonic chord. It is played in the sixth bar, as an alternative to the second bar of Eb7.

In the key of Bb, the bV degree is the note Fb (or E natural for simplicity). Therefore, the progression becomes:

Example 9a:

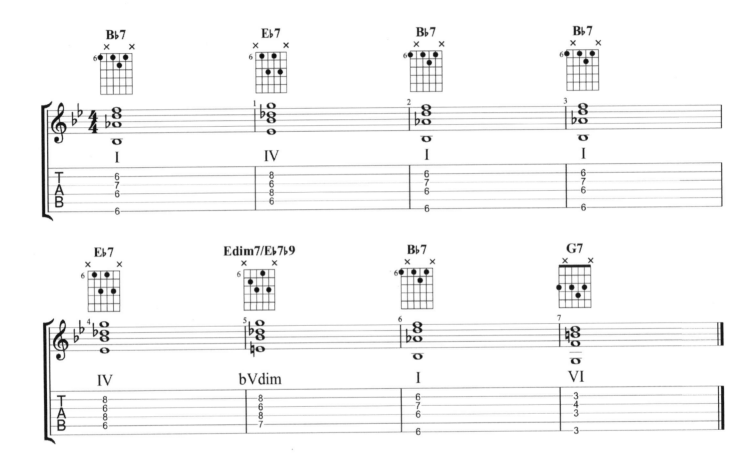

You can play this chord in the following way:

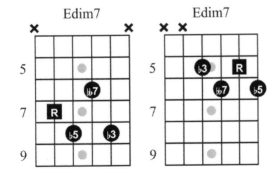

Even though the theory may seem a little intimidating on paper, the truth is that the Edim7 chord still *functions* as an Eb7 chord, albeit with a little more added tension. Here's why:

Look at the notes in *E* diminished 7; (E, G, Bb, Db). When compared to the original Eb7 chord (Eb, G, Bb, Db), you can see that the two chords actually only have one note different between them.

The only difference is that the root of the Eb7 chord has been raised by a semitone to become the note E.

The note E when played over the original Eb root is a b9 interval.

Adding a b9 to a dominant chord is a common alteration in jazz, and sounds great as you can hear in Example 9a.

This explanation may sound a little confusing on paper, so to simplify things, look at the chords of Eb7, and Edim7 written out next to each other:

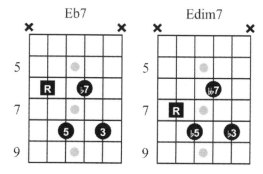

As you can see, the chords are identical except that the bass note has moved up by one semitone.

By adding this tension to bar six of the blues, we create new soloing options that add melodic tension and interest to this point in the progression.

However, there is one easy method to solo over this chord: ignore it!

Because the E diminished chord functions as an Eb7b9 chord, all the Eb7 approaches we already studied will work because the listener is still just 'feeling' an Eb7 chord.

While you should explore this chord using the Eb7 arpeggio and Bebop scale, if we only took that approach, we would miss out on some great soloing opportunities.

The first way to deal with this new chord is to play an E diminished 7 arpeggio over it.

Example 9b:

Edim7 Arpeggio

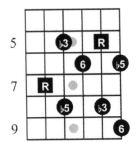

Notice that this arpeggio is identical to the Eb7 arpeggio except that the Eb note has been raised by a semitone to an E. Because the two arpeggios are almost identical, it is effective to target the one changing note, with the Edim7 arpeggio in bar six.

The following examples use 1/4-notes to target the changing arpeggio notes between bars five, six and seven.

Example 9c:

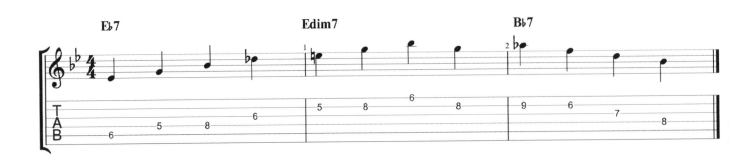

Example 9d:

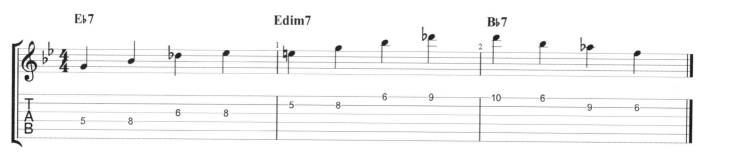

Practice soloing on this chord change just as you did when learning to move from Bb7 to Eb7 in chapters three, four and five.

Be organised. In the above examples, I ascended the arpeggios from the root and 3rd. Repeat this with the 5th and b7th and practice these changes descending. Divide the guitar into two-string groups and focus in great detail on how the chord tones are moving in a small, limited area.

When you are confident with each set of two-string groups, extend the range you are playing to three-string, four-string and five-string groups.

Above all, remember that this is primarily an aural exercise, and training your ears carefully at this stage is what allows you to relax later when you're playing fast solos. You soon be able to just let your ears guide your fingers to the right notes.

When it comes to playing scale-based lines over the Edim7 chord, one of the most appropriate scales to use is the eight note, E Diminished (whole/half scale).

This scale has the formula 1 2 b3 4 b5 #5 6 7. In E, this gives us the notes E, F#, G, A, Bb, C, Db, D#. The Whole-Half Diminished scale is what's known as a *synthetic scale*, because it is not derived from any modal system, such as the modes of the major, harmonic or melodic minor scales.

The Whole-Half Diminished scale is symmetrical: its interval structure *repeats* as can be seen in the following diagram:

E Whole-Half Diminished

Because of this symmetry, the Whole-Half Diminished scale is often used to create melodic patterns and sequences. It is played on the guitar in the following way. The fingerings are a suggestion only.

Example 9e:

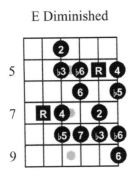

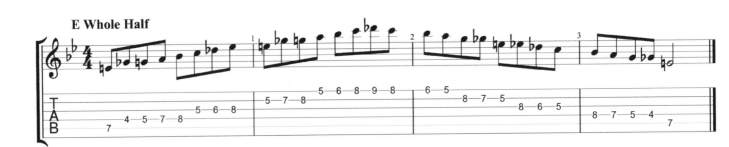

Although this is a unique-sounding scale, it works well over the Edim7 chord, providing you target a chord tone on beat one of the bar.

My favourite note to target is the root, (E) because this is the only note that has been altered from the arpeggio of the previous chord. Targetting the E gives the most obvious melodic effect, as you probably heard in examples 9c and 9d. Another great note to target is the A (b5 of the original Eb chord), as it is another note that clearly defines the change.

The Whole-Half Diminished takes some getting used to, so go slowly, learn to apply it over small string groups, and always target arpeggio notes on the beat.

Learning to apply the E Whole-Half diminished scale was one of my biggest challenges when learning to solo on the jazz blues. It can take a while for this scale to become natural, especially as it is only used for one bar. To get you started, here are some Whole-Half lines you can use over bar six.

Example 9f:

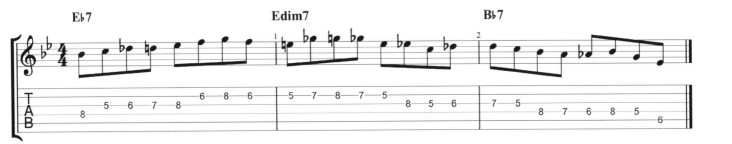

Example 9g:

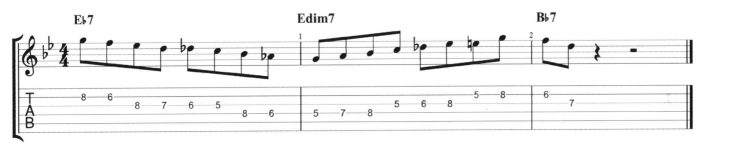

Example 9h:

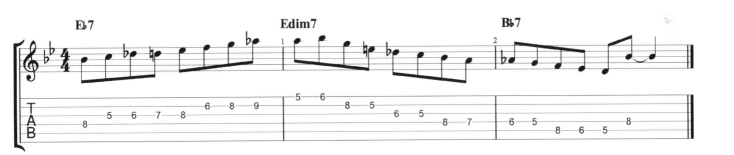

The best way to get used to using the Whole-Half Diminished scale is simply to explore it with a slow backing track.

Chapter Ten - 3rd to 9th Extended Arpeggios

The final concept we will study in this section is the idea of *extended arpeggios*.

The arpeggios we have studied so far have all been played from the root of the chord and ascend 1, 3, 5, b7. A common approach in jazz soloing is to build a new, four-note arpeggio beginning from the *3rd* of the chord.

For example, the arpeggio 1, 3, 5, b7 would be substituted with the arpeggio 3, 5, b7, 9.

The Bb7 arpeggio, Bb, D, F, Ab would be substituted for the notes D, F, Ab and C.

By playing an arpeggio built on the 3rd of the chord, we omit the root and replace it with the 9th of the scale.

Jazz musicians often see the root as an uninteresting note. After all, it is probably being played by other instruments such as the bass or keyboard. The 9th is a stable scale tone and adds a nice richness that works well instead of the root. Of course, this is all a matter of taste, and sometimes you will want to hear the root.

Just remember that the guide tones of any chord (the 3rd and b7) are melodically stronger than the root, and are generally better at articulating chord changes.

Coincidentally, the 3-9 extended arpeggio of Bb7 contains the notes D, F, Ab and C. These are the notes in the arpeggio of Dm7b5. A 3-9 extended arpeggio from the 3rd of a dominant 7 chord, always forms a m7b5 arpeggio.

Once again, this is easier to see in diagram form. Here are adjacent diagrams of the 1-b7 and the 3-9 arpeggios.

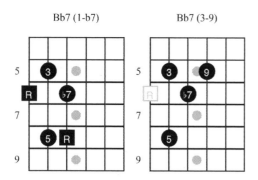

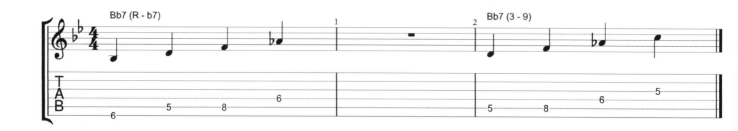

You can play the full extended 3-9 arpeggio in the following way:

Example 10a:

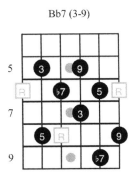

Bb7 (3-9)

(The root is included as a hollow square to help you get your bearings. Don't play it in the arpeggio).

Practice over a loop of Bb7 to Eb7 and target the closest arpeggio note on each chord change. Notice that I am still using the original root-b7 arpeggio on the Eb7 chord.

Example 10b:

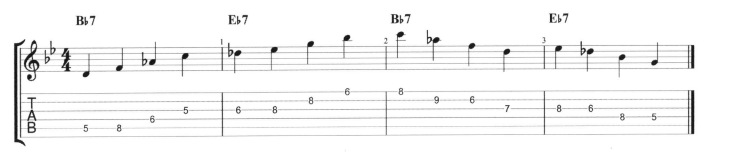

Listen to the difference in melody on the Bb7 chord when you use the 3-9 arpeggio. Can you hear it's richer and more interesting?

Break the guitar neck down into two-string groups and practice nailing the changes between the Bb7 3-9 arpeggio and the Eb7 arpeggio. Do this without a metronome at first so you have time to hear what you're playing. Listen to how the melody feels when you hit the 9th on beat one of the Bb7 bar.

Move your two-string groups across the guitar and gradually increase the numbers of strings in the groupings.

Now let's construct the 3-9 arpeggio for the Eb7 chord.

Once again, playing the 3-9 arpeggio has the effect of replacing the root (Eb), with the 9th of the chord (F). Instead of the notes Eb, G, Bb and Db, (1, 3, 5, b7), we play the notes G, Bb, Db and F (3, 5, b7, 9).

Here are diagrams of the 1-b7, and the 3-9, arpeggios in one octave so that you can compare them.

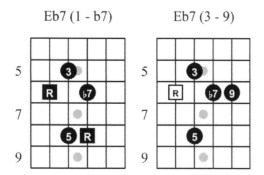

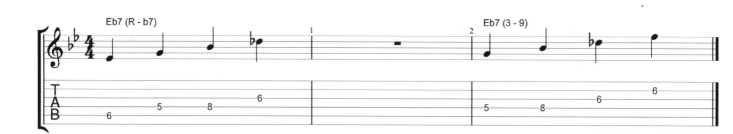

Learn the full arpeggios. Start by focusing on the top four strings as they are more useful for soloing. Leave the bass notes for later.

Example 10c:

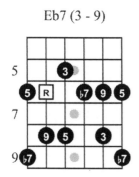

There are two options for practicing this arpeggio: either combine it with the Bb7 arpeggio (1-b7), or combine it with the Bb7 arpeggio (3-9).

If you're confident with the Bb7 (3-9) arpeggio then I recommend jumping straight in and working on the two 3-9 arpeggios together, but feel free to start with the Bb7 (1-b7) arpeggio if you need to.

The following exercise shows how you can target arpeggio tones with both the Bb7 (3-9) and Eb7 (3-9) arpeggios.

Example 10d:

Treat the 9th as an arpeggio tone and practice hitting the changes over small string groups. As this becomes easier, try writing some lines over the chord changes using the chromatic and scale concepts from previous chapters to guide you. Here are some to get you started (9ths are bracketed).

Example 10e:

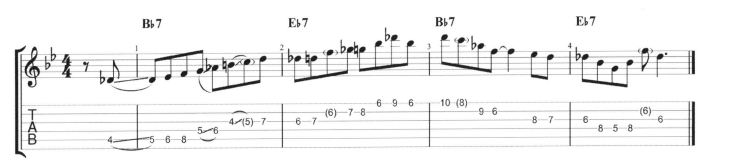

Example 10f:

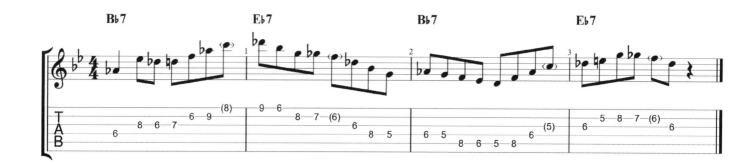

Example 10g:

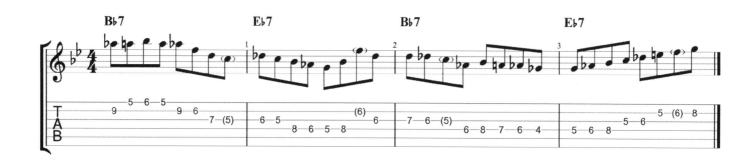

Chapter Eleven - Soloing on Bars Eight to Twelve

We have looked in detail at the most important devices used in jazz guitar soloing and applied them to the first six bars of the jazz blues. The final six bars are more harmonically complex and can be challenging to solo over, but the good news is that we have already prepared most of the groundwork.

Conceptually, soloing over the changes in the final six bars, is identical to soloing over the first six, we just need to learn the appropriate arpeggios and scales to use on these new changes. In its simplest form, soloing over the I VI ii V changes is a case of learning the arpeggios, connecting the dots and adding approach notes. The challenge is that there are now more notes to choose from.

The final bars of a jazz blues consist of two sets of I VI ii V changes, one slow and one quick.

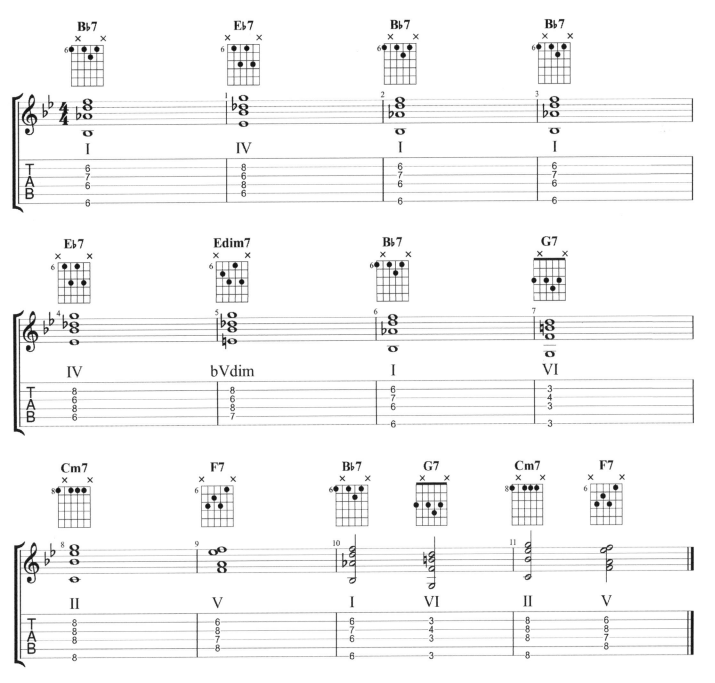

The change from Bb7 to G7 is one of the most important harmonic points in the blues so we will begin by focusing on the transition between these chords. Beginning here also helps join the two sections of the blues progression together smoothly.

We will start by learning the G7 arpeggio on the VI chord in bar eight.

The formula for a Dominant 7 arpeggio is 1 3 5 b7, so from G we get the notes G, B, D and F.

(Begin by focusing only on the notes on the top four strings, and add the hollow bass notes in later).

Example 11a:

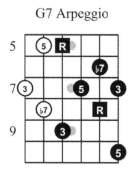

It is important to notice that the G7 chord/arpeggio is not diatonic to the key of Bb and contains the note B Natural. In Chapter One we learnt that the diatonic VI chord in the key of Bb is Gm7, which contains the notes G, *Bb*, D and F.

Because we changed the *quality* of the original Gm7 chord to a dominant 7 (as is standard in a jazz blues), we have introduced the new note, B natural. This pitch is normally completely foreign to the key of Bb, it is a strong, exciting note to target on the G7.

Practice moving from Bb7 to G7, and play arpeggios ascending from the root of each chord. You can use *backing track five* which contains the following loop.

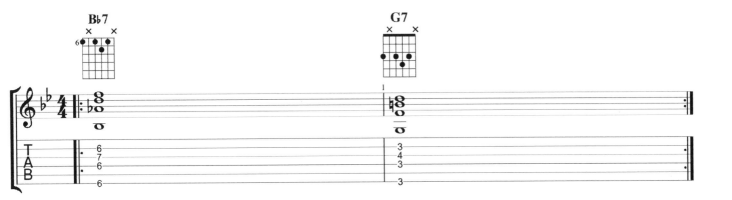

When you can play each arpeggio ascending and descending from the root of each chord, repeat the exercsie from the 3rds, 5ths, and b7s as you learned in Chapter Three. Spend most time on the guide tones, 3 and b7.

Here is one example descending from the b7s of each chord:

Example 11b:

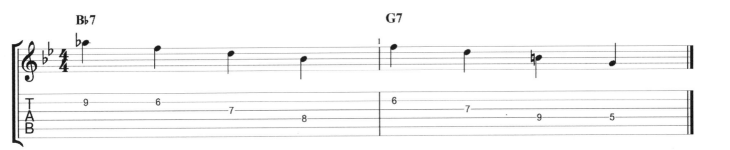

Practice finding the closest changes between the two chords over two-string groups. Here is one possible route on the top two-strings.

Example 11c:

Playing slowly helps you to memorise the fretboard. It's easy to get overwhelmed here as there is a great deal of melodic information.

One bonus is that the 1/4 note pathways you learn here on the slow changes automatically become 1/8th note lines when you apply them to the quick changes in the final two bars. The only goal right now is to learn the neck and internalise the sound of the chords.

Finally, practice changing between the two chords using only guide tones (the 3rd and b7). You will again hear just how powerful the 3rds and b7ths are in defining the sound of any chord.

The following diagrams contain the guide tones of the Bb7 and G7 chords and will help focus your practice on this important sound. Start by playing just one note per bar, then gradually increase the frequency of the notes.

The root is included in the following diagrams for reference only.

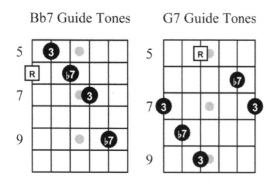

Next, add some simple chromatic approaches to create 1/8th note lines that target arpeggio notes on the beat. Here are some ideas to get you started:

Example 11d:

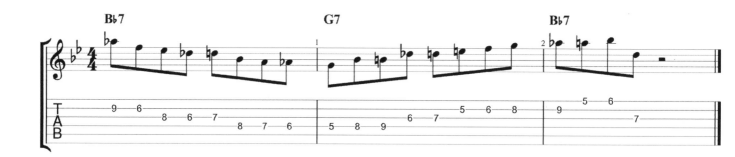

Example 11e:

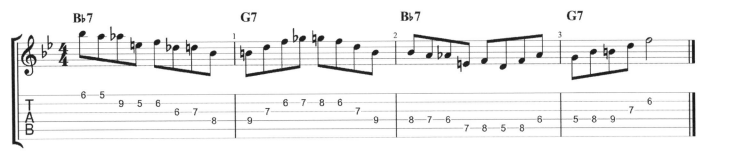

The G7 chord is functioning as a moving dominant 7 chord which resolves to Cm7 in the following bar. For this reason, it's great to add extra tension to the chord by using arpeggio substitutions and altered extensions.

It's important to know we don't always have to play the same arpeggio as the chord (for example G7 arpeggio over a G7 chord). By using other arpeggios, we can create extra tension and interest.

The most common arpeggio substitution on the G7 chord is to play a diminished 7 arpeggio on the 3rd of the chord. The third of G7 is B natural, so the arpeggio substitution we play is B Diminished 7 over G.

The notes of the G7 arpeggio are G, B, D, and F, and the notes of Bdim7 are B D F and Ab. If I re-order the notes, you will see that there is only one note different between the two arpeggios

Arpeggio Interval from G	1	3	5	b7	b9
G7	G	B	D	F	
BDim7		B	D	F	Ab

By playing the arpeggio of Bdim7 over the chord of G7, we omit the root of the chord (G) and replace it with the b9 (Ab).

The harmony we imply with this substitution is G7b9, which is also often played as a chord in the rhythm part. This idea is just like using the Edim7 arpeggio over the implied Eb7b9 chord that you learned in chapter nine.

The b9 is a rich and jazzy interval to play over most functional dominant chords, and it works especially well in the context of a VI dominant chord. There is another advantage too, because the added Ab note is an extra resolution point when the G7 chord moves to Cm7 in the next bar.

You can play the Bdim7 arpeggio in the following way. Just focus on the top four-strings for now.

Example 11f:

G7b9 / Bdim7

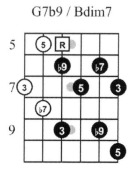

From now on we will always use the G7b9 / Bdim7 arpeggio instead of the G7 arpeggio. This isn't to say that you shouldn't still practice the original G7 arpeggio, but the G7b9 arpeggio is more commonly used and creates a jazzier sound.

Let's practice combining the G7b9 arpeggio with the Bb7 arpeggio. As always, begin by targeting specific intervals on each chord change, i.e., root/b9, 3rds, 5ths and b7s. Remember, G7b9 only has one note different from G7, so you've already worked on most of the note targeting exercises for this chord change.

Here is an example that targets the root of Bb7 and the b9 of G7.

Example 11g:

Now find the closest pathways between the arpeggios too. Here are a few loops of Bb7 to G7 that target the closest adjacent note on each change. Notice that I also use chromatic passing notes and chromatic approach note patterns when appropriate. As always, begin with 1/4 notes and make sure you nail the change on beat one of each bar.

Example 11h:

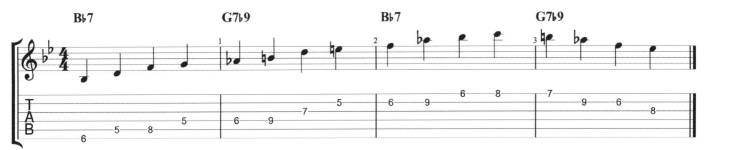

Outlining the change from chord I to chord VI is one of the most distinctive sounds in a jazz blues. The strongest notes to target on the VI chord are the 3rd, the b7 and the b9. When moving from Bb7 to G7, the b7 on the G7 can feel *slightly* weaker as the note (F) is also heard in the Bb7 chord (it is the 5th).

When you can successfully outline the chord change in 1/8th notes using arpeggios, it's time to start using an appropriate scale choice over the G7(b9) chord.

Chapter Twelve - Using the Phrygian Dominant Bebop Scale

A common scale choice on the VI7 chord is the Phrygian Dominant Bebop scale. Just as the Mixolydian Bebop scale is formed by adding a natural 7th to the Mixolydian mode, the Phrygian Dominant Bebop scale is formed by adding a natural 7th to the Phrygian Dominant scale.

The Phrygian Dominant scale has the formula 1 b2 3 4 5 b6 b7. When written with the non-arpeggio notes as extensions the formula is 1 b9 3 11 5 b13 b7.

You'll remember that the b9 interval is why the Bdim7 / G7b9 arpeggio in the previous chapter sounds so good and it is also contained in the Phrygian Dominant scale.

Look at the formula again. The Phrygian Dominant mode contains all the notes of a Dominant 7 arpeggio (1, 3, 5 and b7) plus some beautiful extensions (b9, 11 and b13).

Example 12a:

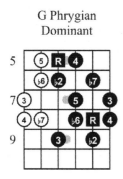

It is important to know this scale, but we want to create an eight-note Bebop scale to keep the arpeggio notes on the beat, just as with the Mixolydian Bebop scale in Chapter Six. This is done by adding a natural 7th between the b7 and the root.

The formula for the Phrygian Bebop scale is 1 b9 3 11 5 b13 b7 7 and is played like this: (the added 'bebop' notes are shown by a hollow dot).

Example 12b:

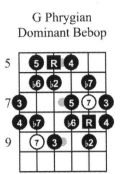

G Phrygian
Dominant Bebop

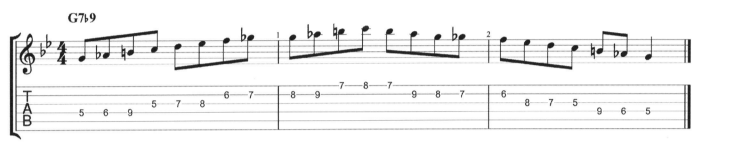

To begin with, this may feel like an awkward fingering for the scale but stick with it.

We can now use this scale to join the dots over the G7 chord. You may now be used to targeting the b9 on the beat of the G7 chord. If you want to use the Bebop scale to keep the arpeggio notes on the beat you must target the root note as the arpeggio note, not the b9.

The b9, as you have heard, does sound great as a target note on the G7 chord, so one way to work with this is to target the b9, but then use a chromatic (bebop) note to place the root back on the beat. More on this later.

Learn the changes between Bb7 and G7 on two-string groups. Use a Bb7 arpeggio on the Bb7 chord and move to the Phrygian Dominant Bebop scale over the G7 chord to begin with. You can reverse this approach so you move from the Bb Bebop scale to a G7b9 arpeggio.

Work towards using Bebop scales over both chords.

Here are some melodic lines on the top four strings to get you started. Work through these concepts slowly and write as many licks as you can. Keep a diary of what you practice and memorise your favourite ideas.

Be methodical in your practice, deliberately begin your lines from the root / b9, 3rd, 5th and b7th of each chord.

Example 12c:

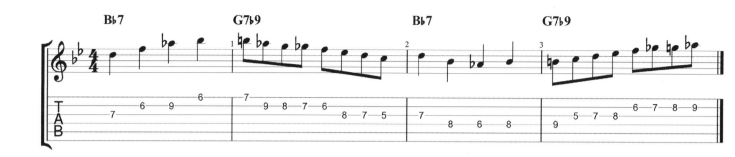

Example 12d:

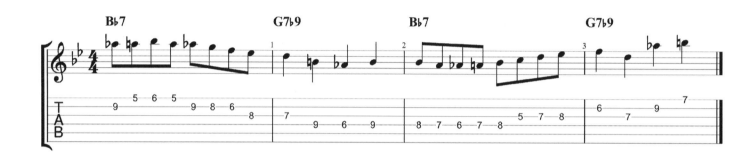

Example 12e:

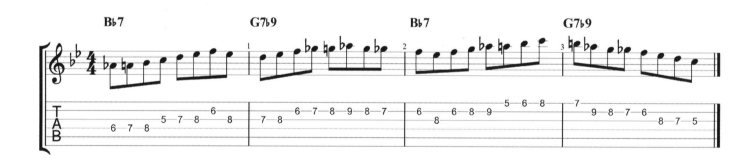

Example 12f:

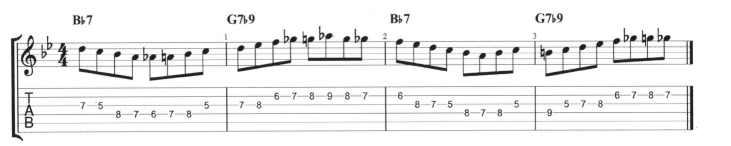

Now let's add in some chromatic passing notes and patterns. Notice in the first example how I target the b9 of G7 and then use a chromatic passing note to put the root back on the beat.

Example 12g:

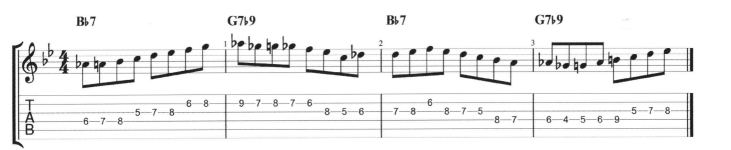

Example 12h

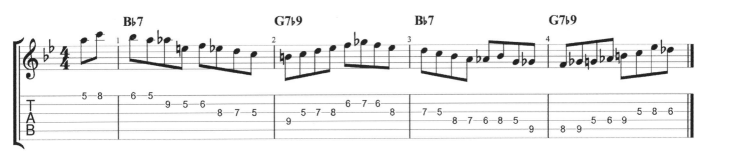

In the next chapter, we will look at moving from the G7 to the Cm7 chord.

Chapter Thirteen - Moving from G7 to Cm7

The final three chords, Cm7, F7 and Bb7 form a ii V I in the key of Bb, so any of the concepts in my book **Fundamental Changes in Jazz Guitar: The Major ii V I for Bebop Guitar**, can be applied here. Be careful though; the blues progression resolves to a dominant 7 chord, not a major 7th chord.

In the jazz blues, it is important to note that the Cm7 chord is often ignored as it comes from the same scale as the F7 chord.

In other words, we can ignore the Cm7 and solo as if it were two bars of F7. We will look at this concept in more detail later, but for now we must start by mastering the appropriate arpeggios to outline the chord changes as articulately as possible.

Here is the arpeggio shape of Cm7. The formula is 1 b3 5 b7 and the notes are C Eb G and Bb.

Example 13a:

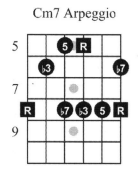

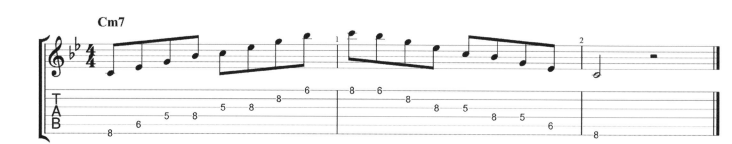

When you have memorised this arpeggio start to play it in conjunction with the G7b9 arpeggio from chapter eight.

Use 1/4-notes and investigate the changing target notes between G7b9 and Cm7 over *backing track six*:

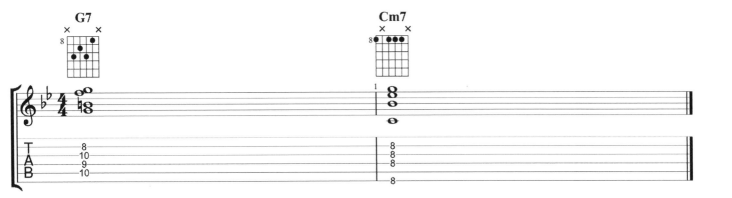

Begin by ascending and descending each arpeggio from the root (or b9th on G7), then from the 3rds, 5ths and b7ths.

These examples will get you started.

Example 13b: *(Ascending from the root/b9)*

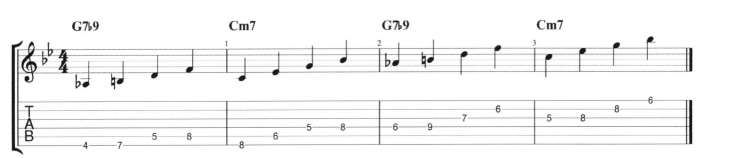

Example 13c: *(Descending from the b7)*

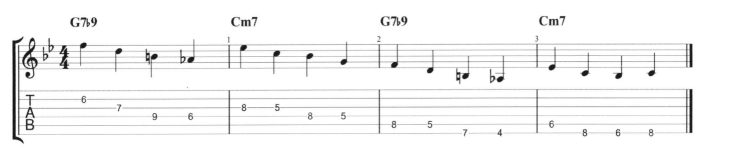

Next, link the arpeggios together by finding the closest target note between the arpeggios. The following examples demonstrate this idea using four-string groups, but again you may wish to begin with two-string groups to develop confidence, aural awareness and fretboard fluency.

Example 13d:

Example 13e:

Now practice linking the Bb7, G7 and the Cm7 chords with arpeggios over *backing track seven*.

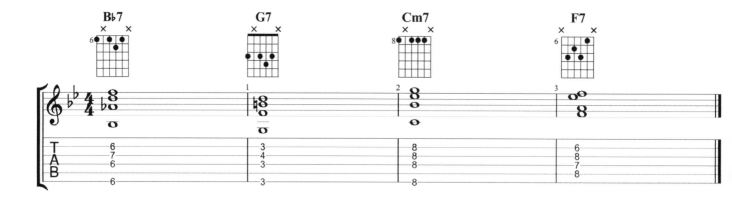

Begin by soloing through the sequence using the 1/4 note arpeggios from the previous chapter, but this time continue into the G7 chord, and stop *on the first note* of the Cm7 arpeggio. Rest on the F7 chord.

Here's just one way you could resolve to the first beat of the Cm7 chord.

Example 13f:

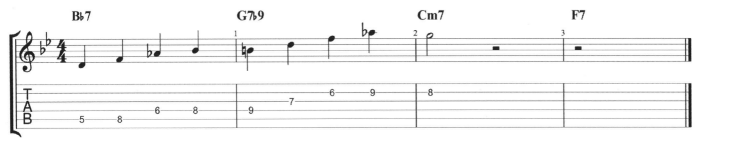

Try the previous exercise without a metronome or backing track to give yourself time to find the right notes. This process is strenuous and mentally demanding to begin with, even at slow speeds.

It is always best to avoid the extra stress caused by the metronome when you're starting out, but the sooner you can practice with a slow click the better.

See how many ways you can resolve to the Cm7 chord. You can also add in some chromatic approach notes on the Bb7 and G7 chords. I hope you can hear how this detailed study quickly builds up to playing articulate jazz lines over changes.

Let's return to working over the G7 to Cm7 change. Now we can add some chromatic passing, and approach notes to the arpeggios. Here are a couple of possibilities.

Example 13g:

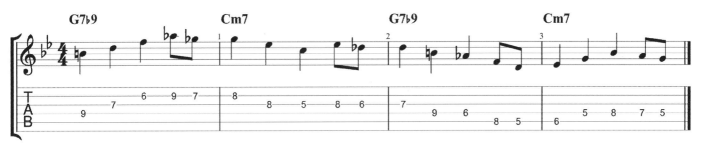

Example 13h:

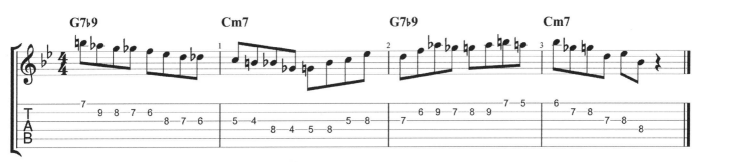

When these arpeggio sounds and a few patterns are solid, it's time to use use the scale which is appropriate to the Cm7 chord: the Dorian Bebop scale.

As I pointed out earlier, a common choice when soloing over the Cm7 chord is to actually use the F Mixolydian Bebop scale, and effectively ignore the Cm7 chord. This is covered in Chapter Sixteen, but for now we will explore the important sound of the C Dorian Bebop scale over the II chord in the turnaround.

Chapter Fourteen - Using the Dorian Bebop Scale

The Dorian Bebop scale is the Dorian mode (formula 1 2 b3 4 5 6 b7) with an added natural 7th this has the formula 1 2 b3 4 5 6 b7 7 , and contains the notes C, D, Eb, F, G, A, Bb, B.

The Dorian Bebop scale can be played in this position in the following way:

Example 14a:

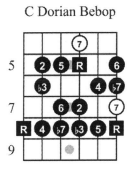

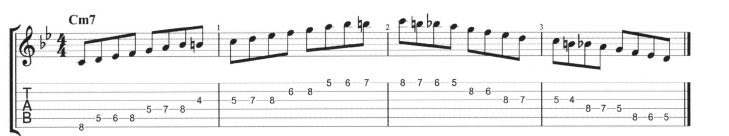

We will learn the C Dorian Bebop scale by using it in combination with the G7b9 arpeggio. Play the G7b9 arpeggio in bar one, and target an arpeggio note of Cm7 in bar two. Continue the line over the Cm7 chord using the Bebop scale.

Example 14b:

Example 14c:

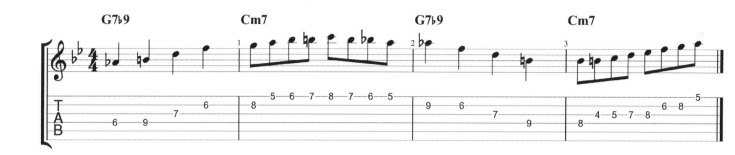

Feel free to add in these chromatic passing notes to help smooth out the changes between the chords.

Explore this concept as much as you can, and be organised in your practice. Deliberately begin from the root/ b9, 3rd 5th and b7th of the G7 chord. Notice how this changes the way you transition into the next chord.

Keep in mind that the point of this exercise is to learn to change *from* G7 *to* Cm7. The exercise will help you learn the opposite movement, but chord VI to II (G7 to Cm7) is a much more common progression than II to VI (Cm7 to G7) in the blues. Don't get too distracted by working on the change from Cm7 to G7, instead of the more important G7 to Cm7. In the blues, the Cm7 will nearly always be followed by an F7 chord.

Next, begin to use the G Phrygian Bebop scale in conjunction with the C Dorian Bebop scale. The following scale ideas are only two bars long. Don't practice moving back to the G7 chord after the Cm7 because you should be starting to focus on the next chord in the sequence, F7.

If you're feeling adventurous, skip ahead to learn the F7 arpeggio and end these lines on the closest arpeggio tone in F7 after the Cm7 bar.

Example 14d:

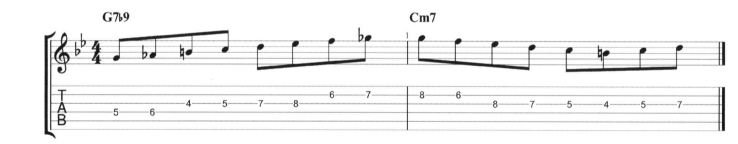

Example 14e:

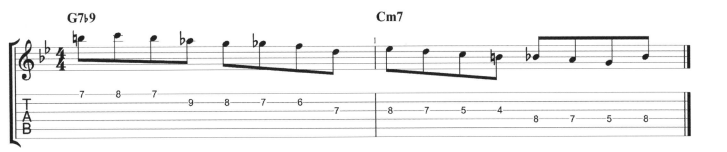

Example 14f:

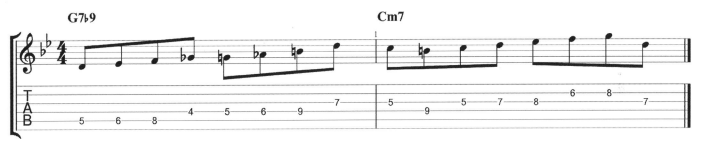

The following lines combine arpeggios with some new chromatic ideas and the Bebop scale. As ever, the most essential element is a strong melodic line that resolves to a chord tone on the beat. On the occasions when I do not play a chord tone on the beat, it is because the note is part of a chromatic approach note pattern.

Example 14g:

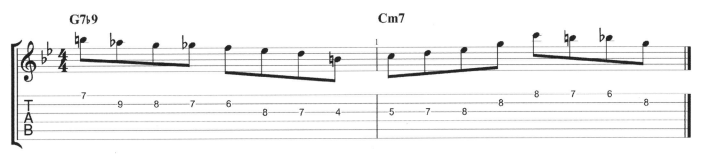

Example 14h:

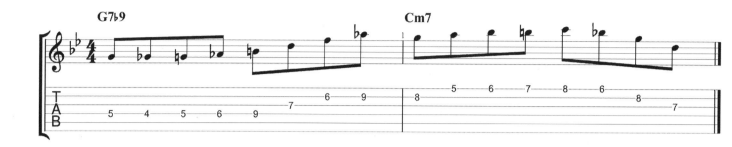

Example 14i:

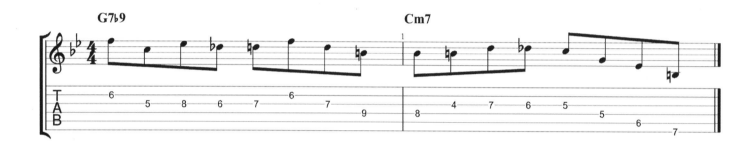

Finally, write some lines that begin from the Bb7 chord. You can play these lines over *backing track seven*. Take a rest on the F7 chord in bar four, but if you know how to, or trust your ears, why not try to land on an arpeggio note of F7 on beat one?

In the following examples, I have made the lines more musical by adding rests and thinking in short phrases.

Analyse each line to see how I have used chromatic notes, bebop scales and arpeggios. Try writing your own lines too.

Example 14j:

Example 14k:

Example 14l:

You can see that even when the notes are sparse, as in Example14l, good voice leading, chromatic approaches and target notes will articulately outline the chords.

Soloing on a jazz blues isn't necessarily about constant streams of bebop 1/8th notes. When we slow down, add space and target the changes, we can hear the blues starting to come out.

Practicing longer lines is essential when developing a bebop vocabulary and learning how the language functions, but don't forget to leave space and listen to the musical effect of the notes you're playing.

In the next chapter we will discuss a number of options available on the F7 chord.

Chapter Fifteen - Soloing on F7

While we can use various scales to solo over each chord in the blues, the dominant chord has the widest variety of scale choices available. Once again, I highly encourage you to pick up a copy of my book **Fundamental Changes in Jazz Guitar: The Major ii V I for Bebop Guitar,** because it goes into much greater depth on the dominant chord than I have room for here.

Let's begin by 'formalising' the most convenient voicing of the full F7 arpeggio.

Example 15a:

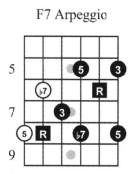

F7 Arpeggio

Begin by ignoring the notes that are lower than the root.

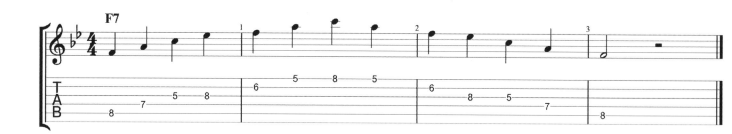

Memorise this arpeggio and when you can play it fluently link it with the Cm7 arpeggio. Remember, the next chord after F7 is Bb7, so you can link from F7 into Bb7 in the same exercise if you like. There is no hurry though!

As always, learn every possible change over small two-string groups using 1/4-notes, before moving onto three- and four-string groups.

These arpeggios are vital for forming a skeleton on which we can hang all melodic ideas. If our ears can always find their way back to an arpeggio tone we won't go far wrong.

Use *backing track eight* to practice the following examples.

Example 15b:

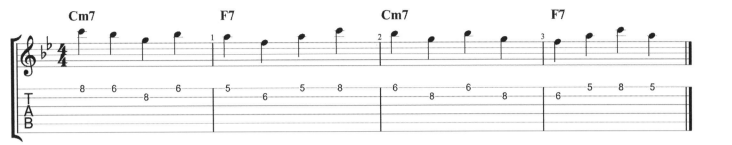

Example 15c:

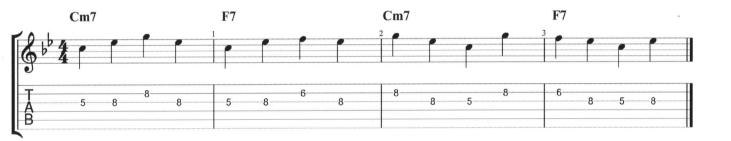

Example 15d: (Backing track nine)

As you can see, there are many permutations of this exercise. By breaking the fretboard down into tiny chunks, we can be thorough in our practice and train our ears.

Just like the G7 chord, the F7 chord is a functional dominant, i.e., it moves to a chord a perfect 5th away. As it is a point of tension in the chord progression, it is normal to create extra tension with interesting arpeggio substitutions and altered scales.

A common arpeggio substitution to use is the diminished 7 arpeggio from the 3rd of the F7 chord (A), creating the same substitution we used over the G7 chord.

Using the diminished 7 arpeggio from the 3rd of F7 (A), gives the notes A, C, Eb and Gb. When we compare these notes to the original notes in the F7 arpeggio we get:

Arpeggio Interval from F	1	3	5	b7	b9
F7	F	A	C	Eb	
A Dim7		A	C	Eb	Gb

Again, we have 'knocked out' the root (F), and replaced it with the b9 (Gb). This creates a slightly tenser feeling over the original F7 chord and adds interest and colour to the solo.

Because the following chord, Bb7 contains the note F, an additional advantage of using this 7b9 substitution is that by playing a Gb over the F7 chord (instead of the original F), we create an extra point of resolution, as the Gb in the F7 chord will fall by step to the F in the Bb7 chord.

This can be seen and heard more easily if I rewrite example 15d to use the Adim7 arpeggio.

Example 15e:

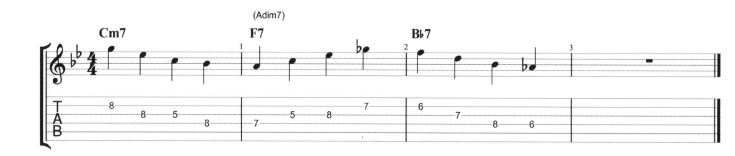

Using the Dim7 arpeggio over the Dominant chord in this way is a common and useful sound. The full Adim7 arpeggio can be played as follows:

Example 15f:

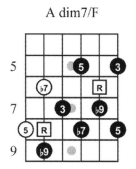

A dim7/F

The root note (F) is shown for reference and should not be played in this example.

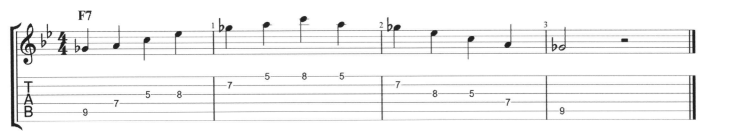

Now repeat all the exercises in this chapter, but this time use the Adim7 arpeggio instead of the F7 arpeggio. Even though there is only one note difference, you will hear a massive change in the way these simple lines sound.

Here is one example played over three strings to help you hear this idea.

Example 15g*:*

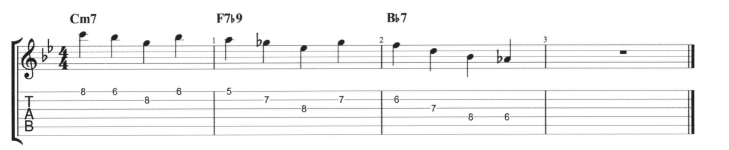

When you gain confidence, try adding the G7b9 arpeggio in bar four of the previous exercise.

Here are a few approach note patterns that target the F7b9 arpeggio and will help you develop a more bebop sound.

Example 15h:

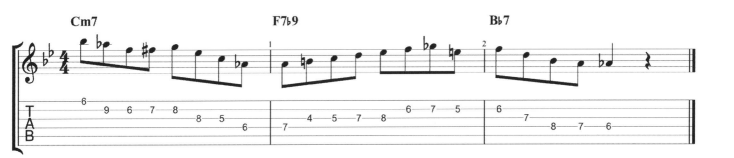

Example 15i:

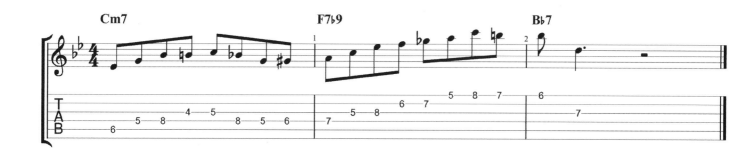

Spend time experimenting with approach note patterns, and writing down your favourite ideas. You can speed them up with a metronome to develop some personalised bebop vocabulary.

Now let's study a common scale choice for the F7 chord.

Chapter Sixteen - The F Mixolydian Bebop Scale

The F Mixolydian Bebop scale works in the same way as the Bb and Eb Bebop scales. It is a Mixolydian scale with an added natural 7th giving the formula 1 2 3 4 5 6 b7 7. The scale of F Mixolydian bebop contains the notes F, G, A, Bb, C, D, Eb, E.

It can be played on the guitar in the following way and the added bebop notes are shown by hollow circles.

Example 16a:

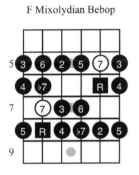

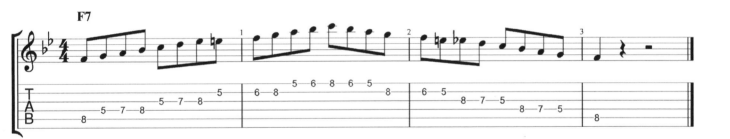

When you have memorised the scale, try a few examples that move from the Cm7 arpeggio into the F Bebop scale before using Bebop scales on both chords. The following examples resolve to an arpeggio note of Bb7.

You can use *backing track eight* to practice the following ideas.

Example 16b:

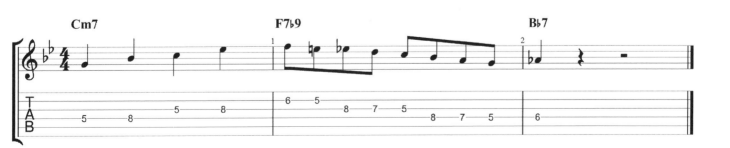

Example 16c:

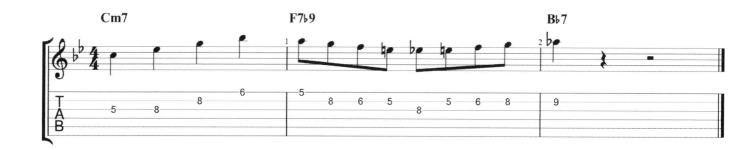

Example 16d:

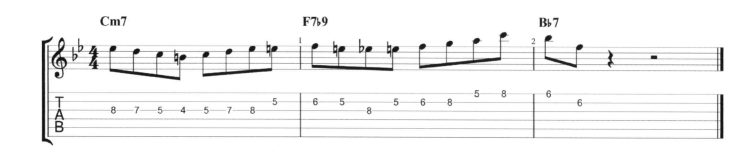

Example 16e:

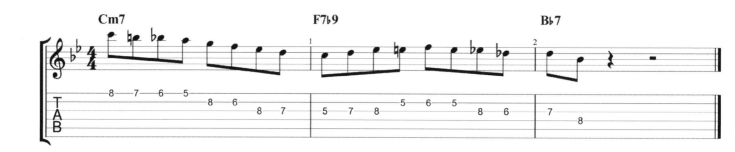

Write your own 1/8th note lines that target arpeggio notes on the change, and be sure to cross the bar line into the Bb7 chord.

I have mentioned already that the F Bebop scale can be used on both the F7 bar and the preceding Cm7 bar. In fact, the arpeggio notes of F7 sound quite good over the Cm7 chord too. For this reason, you often hear jazz musicians ignoring the Cm7 chord and treating it as an extra bar of F7.

This works particularly well at higher speeds, and especially on the quick changes in the final two bars, when having to apply four scales in just eight beats can be a little too intense to be effortlessly musical.

We will discuss how to approach the quick changes later, but for now, here are some lines that use the F Bebop scale over both the Cm7 and the F7 chords. Reverse engineer the lines to see if I'm playing notes from the F7 arpeggio, or Cm7 arpeggio over the Cm7 chord. These lines will sound better at higher speeds.

Example 16f:

Example 16g:

We can add more chromatic ideas, and extend the lines through into the final G7b9 bar, where we will use the G Phrygian Dominant scale combined with the Bdim7 arpeggio.

The following lines have all been constructed from the melodic concepts covered in the book so far.

Example 16h:

Example 16i:

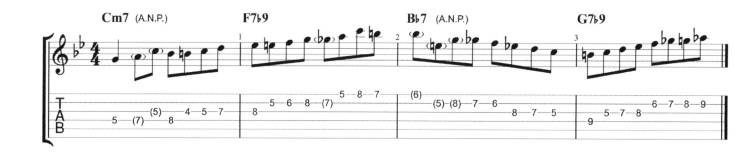

* A.N.P. = approach note pattern.

Remember, you don't have to play long lines of 1/8th notes.

Example 16j:

One strategy you can use to build different phrase lengths is to start the line on a specific beat of each bar. For example, play from beat two, three or four. You can also start on an off-beat, by beginning the line with a chromatic approach note or a scale tone. The next example begins on the off-beat of beat two.

Example 16k:

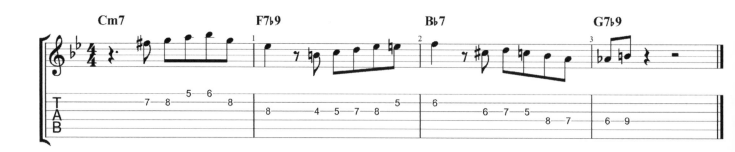

Of course, you don't have to begin on beat two of every bar, and you can always miss out complete bars entirely. Experiment with different phrase lengths: try four, five, six or seven-note phrases that cross the bar lines.

Remember that the changes on the jazz blues are actually:

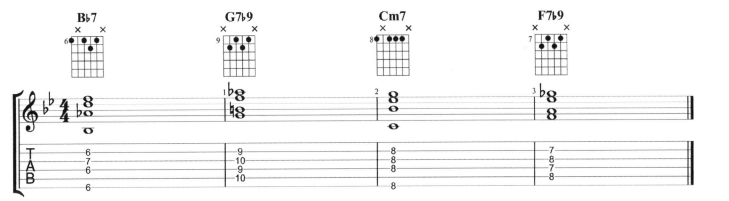

Not the sequence beginning with Cm7 above.

You should now practice soloing on this actual chord sequence along with *backing track ten*. The work you have done so far is instantly transferable to this progression.

Chapter Seventeen - The F Altered Scale

The F Altered scale is one of the more dissonant, 'out there' scales that jazz musicians commonly use. It can be seen as a dominant 7 arpeggio with every possible chromatic alteration to a dominant 7 chord added. The important thing to notice is that this scale does *not* contain a natural 5th which gives the Altered scale a tense, unsettled feeling.

I could (and probably will) write a whole book on the applications of the altered scale but for now let's look at some purely scalic ways to approach this important sound.

The formula for the altered scale is 1 b9 #9 3 b5 #5 b7.

The notes in the F Altered scale are F, Gb, G#, A, Cb, C#, Eb.

As mentioned, the scale contains the 1, 3 and b7 of the dominant 7 chord, but with all the possible alterations; b9, #9, b5 and #5. (You will often see a #5 interval described by its enharmonic spelling *b13*).

There is no natural 5th in the scale.

Notice that the Altered Scale contains the Adim7 (F7b9) arpeggio we used in Chapter Fifteen. This is a strong sound and a good starting point for any improvisation.

The intervals lay out on the guitar neck like this:

Example 17a:

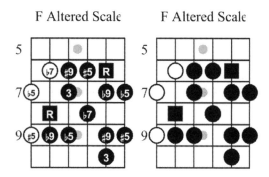

I have included two fretboard diagrams: one with the intervals of the scale included, and one without so it's easier to read.

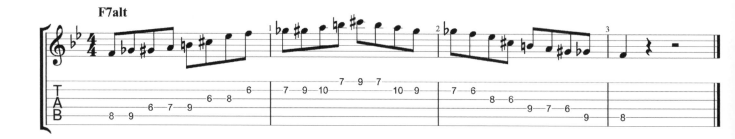

As the V7 (F7) chord is one of the strongest points of tension in the blues progression, it is perfectly fine to add extra tension by using the Altered scale, even if some of the notes clash slightly with the underlying harmony.

The secret to making the altered scale work is to make the resolution obvious when you return to the I chord (Bb7). Using triad and arpeggio figures derived from the Altered scale is also a strong approach.

The easiest way to begin is by playing an altered scale idea that resolves to a chord tone of Bb7. Right from the start, you may find that you need to add chromatic notes to help create a smooth transition. Play 1/4 notes over the following progression, sticking to two-string or three-string groupings. Target arpeggio tones on the Bb7 chord, but don't worry too much about hitting arpeggio notes on the F7 altered chord. Use *backing track eleven*.

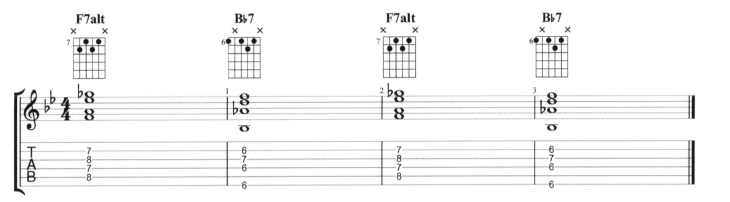

Here are a few ideas played on two-string groups to get you started.

Example 17b:

Example 17c:

These exercises normally take a while to absorb – partly because the notes are new, but also because many of the dissonances you create are an acquired taste. Keep playing along with the backing track and allow your ears to become accustomed to these new colours.

Next, add in the ii chord; Cm7. Play arpeggio notes on the first beat of the Cm7 and Bb7 bars, and move to the closest note of the F Altered scale on the F7 chord. For now, take a rest on the G7b9 chord.

Use *backing track nine* to practice these ideas.

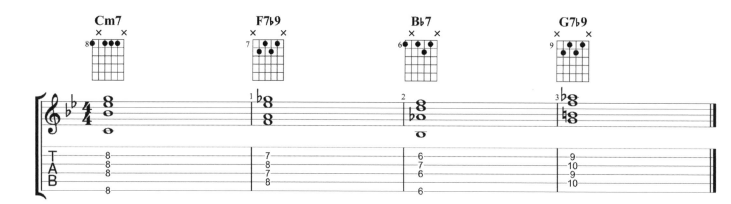

The following examples use three-string groups, although you may wish to begin with two-string groups to build confidence and fluency.

Example 17d:

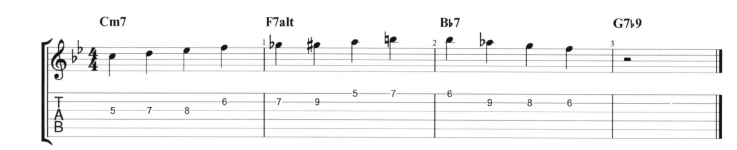

Example 17e:

Next add in the G Phrygian Dominant scale on G7.

In the following example, I use the three-string grouping on the 4th, 3rd and 2nd strings. You can start with two-string groups if you need to.

Example 17f:

Example 17g:

This process may seem long winded, but you only need to do it once. In fact, because of the detail in which you study the neck, it is much quicker to take this approach. The goal is total fretboard fluency and aural awareness in this position.

Let's make some 1/8th note lines from the F Altered scale. In the following examples, I use chromatic approach notes when I need to.

Notice I am now using the original I VI ii V progression from the blues *backing track ten*.

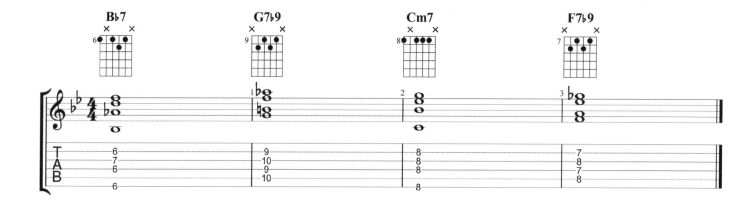

Example 17h:

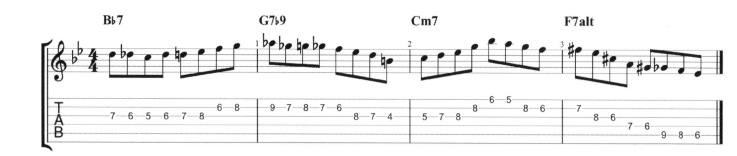

Example 17i:

Example 17j:

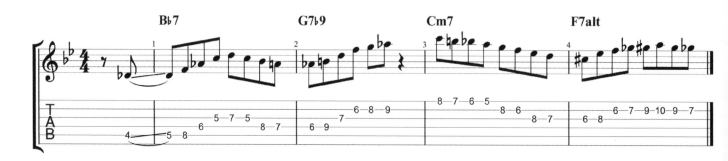

These examples will get you started, but the Altered scale is tricky to use if you haven't already spent time developing your arpeggio skills over the other chords.

Above all, go slowly. Locking the sound in your ears by playing accurate 1/4 notes at 40bpm will get you playing intricate jazz lines more quickly than rushing in with fast 1/8ths at 180bpm. You should think of this approach as a big game of dot to dot: you're linking the arpeggio 'dots' with lines made from the scale and approach notes.

The F Altered sound is common and you will hear it often. The secret to making it work is hear a good resolution point in the following bar.

As you get better, you will find yourself taking more liberties, and playing scale tones and even chromatic alterations on the beat. Your ability to do this depends completely on your ears, and how well you can resolve a tension.

Chapter Eighteen - Practicing Quick Changes

The final two bars in a jazz blues are a condensed repeat of the preceding four bars. The same chords are played with two chords per bar.

The sequence is:

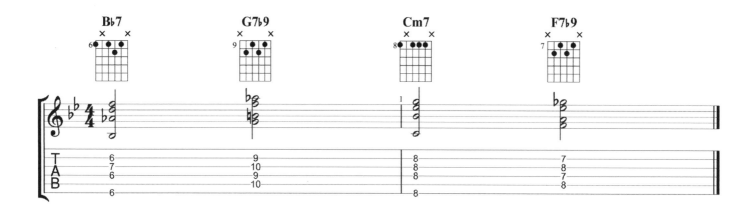

This can be heard on *backing track twelve.*

The good news is that you have already done the preparation and groundwork for this sequence because of your detailed study in the previous chapters.

You have played over these chord changes with 1/4 note lines. Now that each chord only lasts two beats, you can simply double the speed of the 1/4 note lines to instantly create 1/8th note lines. Here's how the 1/4 note rhythms over four bars double up into 1/8th notes over two bars.

Example 18a:

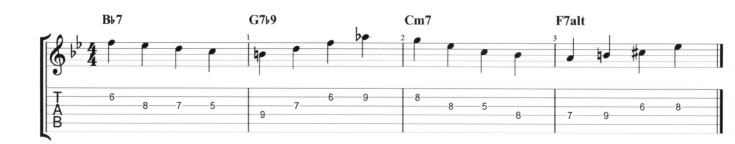

Condensed, this becomes:

Example 18b:

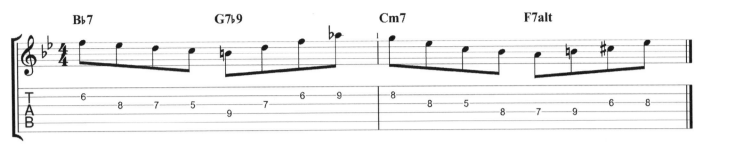

To practice soloing over quick changes, the following exercises are useful.

First, play just arpeggios (you can use 7b9 arpeggios if you like) and play one note per chord.

In the following examples, I show just one possible route around the changes, but there are hundreds. Spend time consolidating this section and finding as many paths as you can. This will train both your ears and your fretboard knowledge.

Begin with targeting guide tones (3rds and 7ths).

Example 18c: *(just 3rds)*

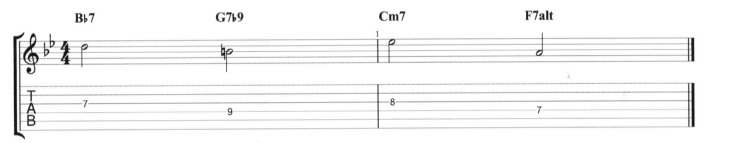

Example 18d: *(just 7ths)*

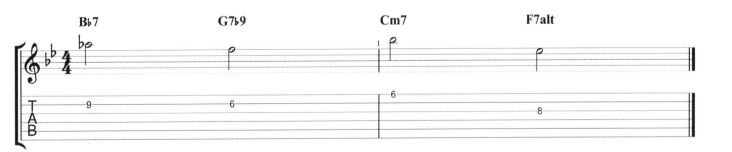

Example 18e: *(both 3rds and 7ths)*

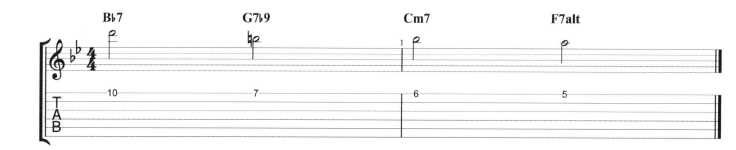

When you're confident you can hit just 3rds, just 7ths, or any combination of the 3rds and 7ths in both octaves, begin targeting the closest note available note in the next arpeggio.

Example 18f:

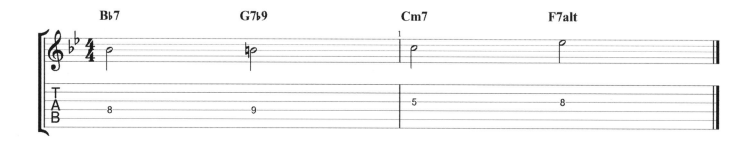

Example 18g:

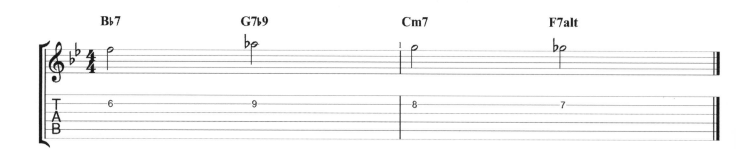

Next, try playing two notes on each chord and repeat the process.

Example 18h: *(guide tones)*

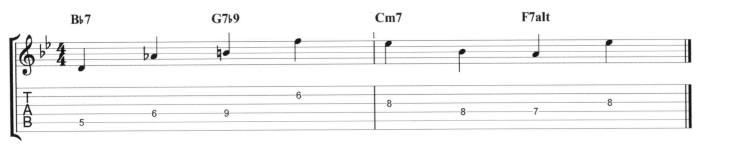

Example 18i: *(closest note)*

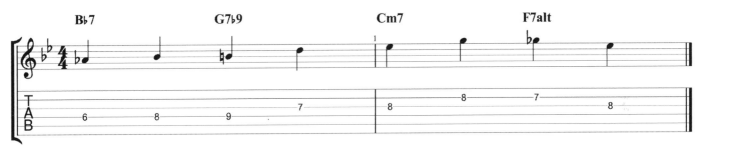

Now add a chromatic approach note a semitone below each arpeggio tone:

Example 18j:

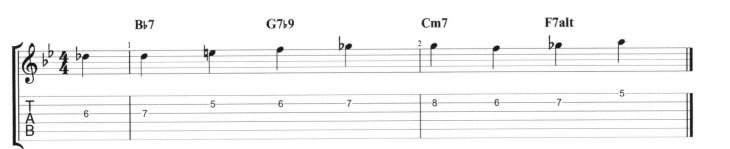

Let's work towards 1/8th note lines by adding in 1/8th notes on beats two and four.

Example 18k:

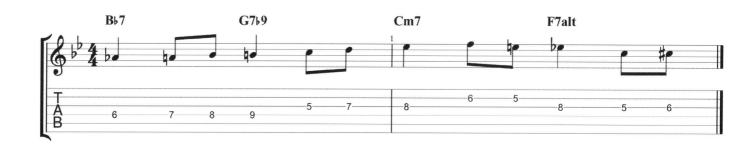

Example 18k is an essential exercise for learning to hit target notes over quick changes. By forcing yourself to play the correct chord-scale in a set rhythm and hit an arpeggio note on every chord change, you begin to think and process melodic information quickly and accurately.

Go slow. Set your metronome to 40bpm and see how long you can play ideas based on Example 18k. The idea is to play target notes on beats one and three, and fill in beats two and four with 1/8th notes taken from the correct scale or chromatic approach notes.

Split this exercise into two parts, one where you *only* play scale notes on beats two and four, and one where you *only* play chromatic approach note patterns on beats two and four. This will help you get great of mileage out of this simple concept.

After a while, change the rhythms of the notes that you play on beats two and four. You could use triplets or 1/16th note ideas.

This exercise will cement the sound of the target notes in your ears and allow you to work at fast tempos. The key is to force yourself to stick with the exact same rhythm throughout the process.

Let's now look at a few lines that are constructed with only 1/8th notes.

Example 18l:

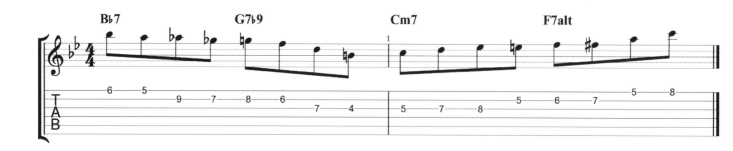

Example 18m:

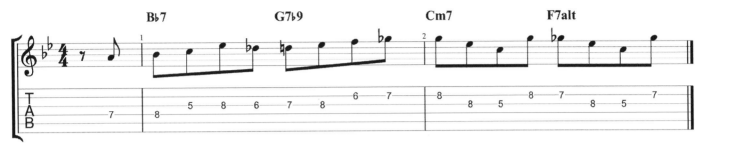

Example 18n:

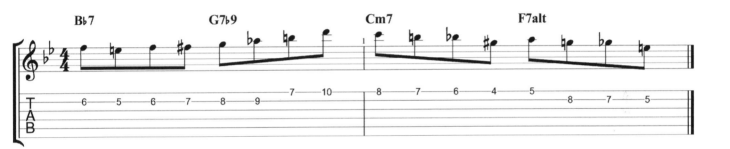

As always, reverse engineer these lines to see how I place each arpeggio note on the beat and fill in the gaps with melodic ideas.

Spend time writing your own quick I VI ii V lines in 1/8th notes.

Chapter Nineteen - Pentatonic Scales

A book on Jazz-blues guitar would not be complete without a section on using pentatonic scales.

Although I stated in the introduction that I would expect a reader of this book to have a decent grasp of using the Minor Pentatonic scale, it is used differently in a jazz blues, than a Texas style blues.

Many great players, such as George Benson, make much more use of the *Major* Pentatonic Blues scale than they do the Minor Pentatonic scale. The minor pentatonic is, of course, used too, but a large part of the jazz sound comes from combining the major blues scale with the chord tone approaches we have studied in this book.

Here is one way to play the Bb Major Pentatonic Blues scale:

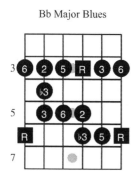

Example 19a:

You may notice that this scale looks identical to the G Minor Pentatonic Blues scale.

I have written it slightly out of position in relation to the rest of the book as most guitarists are much more comfortable playing the scale in this way.

To begin, try using the Bb Major Blues scale over the whole blues progression, and play in phrases based around 1/8th notes. Avoid bending the strings and adding vibrato.

Here are a few jazzy pentatonic lines to get you started. When you're playing these, *think* G Minor Pentatonic:

Example 19b:

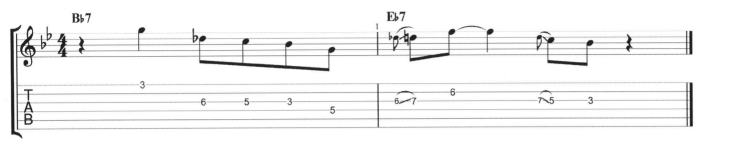

Example 19c:

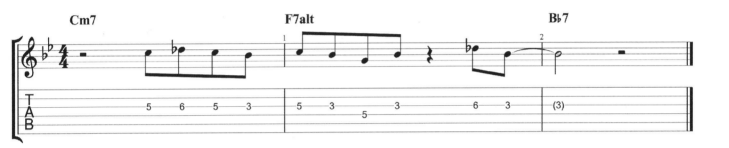

Example 19d:

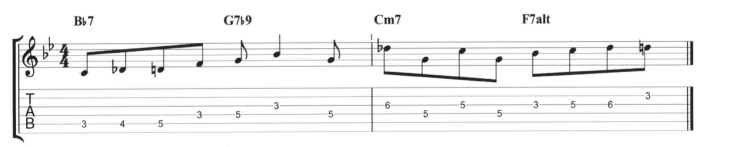

What you will find by experimenting, is that the Bb Major Blues scale tends to work over some areas of the jazz blues better than others. With clever placement of your notes (think about targeting arpeggio tones), you can make it work nearly everywhere, but if it's not coming quickly, try switching to the Bb Minor Pentatonic (blues) scale where you find it difficult.

You can move any Bb Major Blues scale lick up three frets and it instantly becomes a Bb Minor Blues scale idea. This works well when moving from Bb7 to Eb7 in either bar two or bar five.

Example 19e:

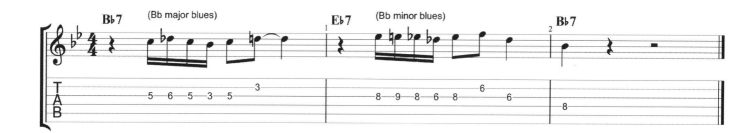

The natural tendency for most players is to use the major and minor blues scales on the first seven bars of the jazz blues, and change back to chord tone 'bebop' soloing on the final five. This is a great strategy to begin with and you should spend time exploring that as a soloing scheme, however it is also useful to practice the reverse too.

By over-practicing pentatonic blues ideas on the first seven bars and 'bebop' on the second five, it is easy to play a segmented jazz blues solo that doesn't necessarily hang together as a complete musical statement.

To counter this, I advise you to spend time practicing chord tone 1/8 note lines on the Bb7 to Eb7 section and using the blues scale ideas in the final five bars. Both approaches will combine naturally, and you will soon find yourself playing pentatonic based ideas that target chord tones to articulate the changes, wherever you are in the progression.

For more information about pentatonic approaches to blues soloing, I would suggest checking out my books **The Complete Guide to Playing Blues Guitar Book Two: Melodic Phrasing**, and **Book Three: Beyond Pentatonics**, which are both available from Amazon and Fundamental-Changes.com

While both books were primarily written for traditional Texas-style blues playing, all of the phrasing and conceptual ideas can easily be adapted to the jazz blues.

N.B. The scale shape I have given for the Bb Major Blues Pentatonic scale above is not in the same fretboard position as all the other scale diagrams in this book. This is because most guitarists instantly recognise and play this shape well. If you wish to use the Bb Major Blues scale in the same position as all the other ideas in this book, you can use this shape:

Bb Major Blues

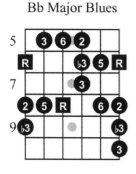

Chapter Twenty: Jazz Blues Solo Examples

The following two choruses are an improvised solo, using many of the techniques and approaches in this book.

Example 20a:

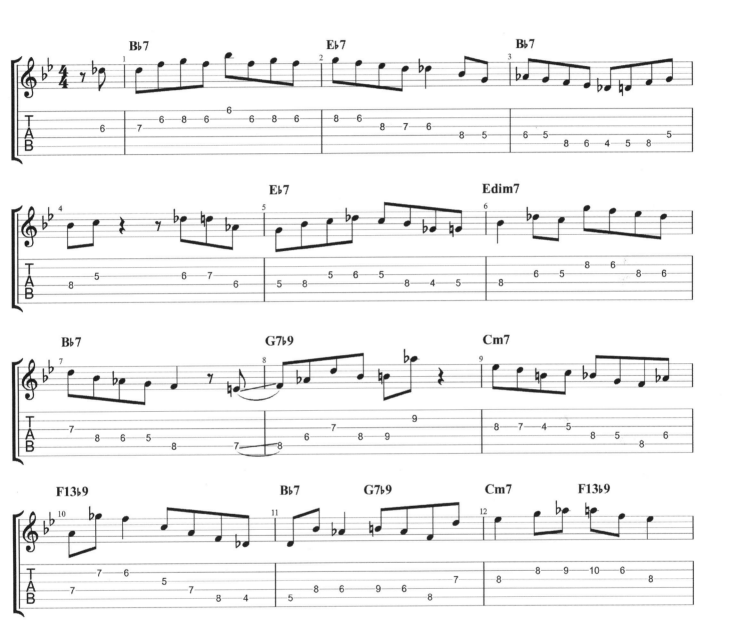

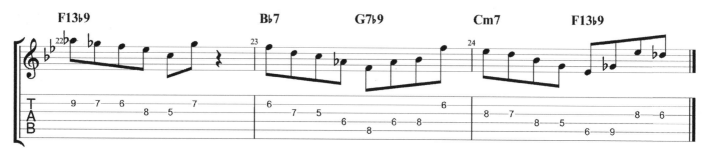

Conclusions, Practice Tips and Further Study

I have tried to cram as many musical ideas and concepts into this book as possible. There is enough here to get you soloing articulately over a jazz blues and should keep you busy for a long time. I hope you can now hear and understand the different approaches a jazz musician takes on a blues and begin to incorporate these ideas into your own playing.

The key to success is structured, focused practice. I would recommend only working on two or three concepts concurrently. Practice each one for twenty, focused minutes, take a ten-minute break (leave the room, walk around), then focus on a completely different part of the blues. A typical practice session my look like this:

- 20 minutes: Comping rhythm on top four-string chords with a metronome at 40 bpm. Increase speed if fluent

- 10 minutes break: Go outside, see family, drink water

- 20 minutes: 1/4-note exercises over quick I VI ii V section at 50 bpm

- 10 minutes: Stretch

- 20 minutes: Write Bb Major Blues scale lines for the Bb7 chord. 90bpm

Take your breaks away from the room where you practice. Keep a diary of your practice and spend a minute after your practice session to write down what you achieved and where you will begin tomorrow.

If you're not feeling great about your 20-minute practice session, *stop*. Take a break and approach it fresh tomorrow. You'll be surprised how much gets processed unconsciously in your breaks.

Stay off the computer! No Facebook, Instagram or Twitter. Turn your phone off when you practice too!

Practice both with backing tracks and just the metronome. When you are working with only a click, you should be able to hear the chord changes implied by your melodic solo line.

One final note.

The best thing you can do to understand how the concepts in this book are applied musically, is to transcribe and analyse solos by the great jazz musicians. Listen to your favourite players and work out their ideas. Analyse them before incorporating them into your own playing.

Good Luck!

Joseph

Other Books from Fundamental Changes

Chord Tone Soloing for Jazz Guitar

Complete Technique for Modern Guitar

Fundamental Changes in Jazz Guitar

Guitar Chords in Context

Guitar Finger Gym

Guitar Fretboard Fluency

Guitar Scales in Context

Jazz Blues Soloing for Guitar

Jazz Guitar Chord Mastery

Minor ii V Mastery for Jazz Guitar

Sight Reading Mastery for Guitar

The Circle of Fifths for Guitarists

The Complete Guide to Playing Blues Guitar Compilation

The Complete Jazz Guitar Soloing Compilation

The First 100 Jazz Chords for Guitar

The Jazz Guitar Chords Compilation

The Melodic Minor Cookbook

The Practical Guide to Modern Music Theory for Guitarists

Voice Leading Jazz Guitar

100 Classic Jazz Licks for Guitar

Modern Jazz Guitar Concepts with Jens Larsen

Martin Taylor Beyond Chord Melody

Printed in Great Britain
by Amazon